Blood Sweat and Tears

A Play

John Godber

A SAMUEL FRENCH ACTING EDITION

SAMUEL FRENCH

FOUNDED 1830

SAMUELFRENCH-LONDON.CO.UK
SAMUELFRENCH.COM

FOR AMATEUR PRODUCTION ENQUIRIES

UNITED KINGDOM AND WORLD EXCLUDING NORTH AMERICA

plays@SamuelFrench-London.co.uk

020 7255 4302/01

Each title is subject to availability from Samuel French,

depending upon country of performance.

BLOOD SWEAT AND TEARS

First performed by Hull Truck Theatre Company at the
Spring Street Theatre in Hull in a production with the
following cast:

Louise Underwood	Jane Clifford
Michele Gray	Gill Tompkins
Sarah Goodwin	Liza Sadovy
Stuart Mason	Mick Callaghan
Andy Brookes	Steve Brough

Directed by John Godber

This re-written version was premièred by Big Telly
Theatre Company in 1993 in a production directed by Zoë
Seaton

SYNOPSIS OF SCENES

ACT I

SCENE 1	*Pippins* Burger Bar. Winter. Evening
SCENE 2	Judo hall. Later the same evening
SCENE 3	*Pippins*. Four days later. Morning
SCENE 4	Judo hall. Some days later. Evening
SCENE 5	Judo hall. Some days later. Evening
SCENE 6	Judo hall. The following week. Evening
SCENE 7	Judo hall. Some days later. Evening

ACT II

SCENE 1	Judo hall. Some time later. Evening
SCENE 2	Judo hall. Some days later. Evening
SCENE 3	An empty space. Evening
SCENE 4	Judo hall. Later. Evening
SCENE 5	Judo hall. Some days later. Evening

CHARACTERS

Stuart Mason Stuart is forty-one. He works in a semi-skilled job and has dedicated most of his life to judo. He was trained in the old style of judo — that is, he was taught to do month after month of break-falling — however, he doesn't teach in this way. He is a simple man, warm and generous, hassled yet in control. He is only too aware that the club is subject to council governing and realizes that the larger local sports centre will eventually take his best players. In an attempt to attract players he advertises self-defence classes.

Andy Brookes Andy is in his mid-twenties. He is a Black Belt First Dan. He is the local Humberside champion. He is an attractive man who cuts a dashing figure. He is always in the local paper, and, from a large council estate, he is a model for escape. His judo has taken him all over the world. He has a stoicism that is common amongst Black Belts but will never be the world champion because of an inherent laziness. One should feel that Andy has been saved from himself by judo; without judo he may well have fallen foul of society.

Sarah Goodwin Sarah is in her early twenties. At the beginning of the play she is a Blue Belt, and is the Lincoln and Humberside women's champion. She will never aspire to any other championship but it is enough for her that she is the champ. She has been going steady with Andy Brookes for about two years and wants to get engaged. Most of the time, however, he is away training in London and her job as a policewoman doesn't allow her much time off. She has been in the police force since school. She is a very curt person, and plays everything right down the line. She seldom talks about the police side of her work but we know she is proud of it and is aware of the paradoxes that police work today presents. She has no real loyalty to Stuart and his *dojo*; indeed the police have a training instructor of their own and at times she trains with him. She was Head Girl at Greatoak High School where she did fairly well with A levels. She would have been studious rather than imaginative. A good all-round athlete, she is generally intolerant of other people's shortcomings. She is probably destined to make a career from the police force.

Michele Grey Michele is in her early twenties. She is not a Black Belt in judo, and will never be. At the beginning of the play she is probably just twenty. She left school with four CSE Grade Ones; she is of above average intelligence, but she is twenty going on thirty-five. She is an attractive and likeable character, off the wall and streetwise. She has never done any exercise in her life except perhaps on an "18 to 30" holiday with the Greek and Spanish waiters. Whorish in a way but still with a schoolgirl's innocent giggle, she is easy prey for the smart young man with car keys. She works in the local fast greasy food shop *Pippins*. Even at work she is adorned with some of the most outrageous ear-rings and nail varnish. In this dead end job, she sees the only possible escape is in catching a "fella", getting a baby and settling down. She appreciates how depressing a prospect this is but can see nothing else for her. She is not a good catch; hence she is still looking. She has a boyfriend, Gary Spencer, who regularly hits her; neither would say it was a serious relationship. She was at school with Louise Underwood who lives around the corner on their estate, and has been Louise's best friend for years.

Louise Underwood Louise is twenty at the beginning of the play. As a younger girl she was a handful; from a family with two brothers, she was something of a tomboy. She is not unattractive but looks ordinary in a crowd. With only a handful of qualifications she saw the job at *Pippins* as a good opening and has been there four years. She has had boyfriends on and off, but nothing to shout about. She lives on the same estate as Andy Brookes and is intelligent enough to realize that he has escaped from the mundanity of everyday existence. She has a good sense of humour and finds it difficult to take many things too seriously. She doesn't realize that she has the capacity to absorb. She gets into the judo almost despite herself. The acquisition of a judo belt is a great achievement for someone who asks for very little. It is an enormous personal sacrifice to lose a very close friend in order to gain her self-satisfaction. As a character the audience need to be with her and associate with her entirely throughout the play.

AUTHOR'S NOTE

A glossary of the judo terms used in the play

Dojo	a training hall
Hajime	start; a referee's call to start a contest
Hari goshi	sweeping loin throw
Ippon Sieonage	a winning throw by *Sieonage* (shoulder throw)
Judogi	clothes worn when competing
Matte	wait; a refereeing term
Osoto gari	a major outer reaping throw
Ouchi gari	a major inner reaping throw
Randori	free practice
Tiaotoshi	a body throw
Tomenage	a stomach throw
Uchikomi	a repeating exercise
Ukemi	a break fall

Scores

Ippon	a winning throw; 10 points
Waza ari	almost *Ippon*; 7 points
Yuko	almost *Waza ari*; 5 points
Koka	almost *Yuko*; 3 points

Other plays by John Godber published by
Samuel French Ltd:

April in Paris
Happy Families
Salt of the Earth
Teechers
Up 'n' Under
Up 'n' Under II

ACT I

SCENE 1

A city in the north of England. Winter. Evening

A composite set on two levels. On the higher level UR *is* Pippins, *a downmarket type of burger bar. (In* ACT II *this level is used for Michele's speech.) Occupying most of the stage is the* dojo, *a judo hall, which is extremely run down. In the centre of the hall is a large square of judo matting. On the wall are poster reminders of what the club was like in its golden period. Battered lockers, broken chairs and splintered benches surround the mats. There is an exit to a distinctly uninviting-looking shower area*

As the CURTAIN *rises, the* Lights *are up on* Pippins *only. A number of the tables are untidy. Louise and Michele, dressed in their* Pippins *waitress uniforms, wearily clear away the debris of another day. Michele is particularly slovenly in her approach to the job, lighting a cigarette and smoking throughout the following scene. Louise is doing most of the work, wiping tables and mopping the floor during the following*

Michele Chuffin' knackered.
Louise You what?
Michele Knackered.
Louise Been busy.
Michele Burger mad.
Louise Who?
Michele In here.
Louise Cheap, that's why.
Michele I don't eat 'em, I don't like 'em. You don't know what you're eating.
Louise It's just meat, i'n't it?
Michele Burger mad in here. Bloody animals. It's like a chuffin' zoo in here if you ask me.
Louise Cheap though, i'n't it?
Michele Cheap and nasty.
Louise Like you.
Michele Like you.
Louise Thanks.

Michele Oh, look.

Louise What?

Michele Look at me heels. Just look at them. I'm cut to ribbons.

Louise Cheap shoes.

Michele You what, you cheeky sod — these aren't cheap.

Louise Cheap shoes. Plastic does that to me.

Michele Twelve quid these, in the sale.

Louise You need a plaster.

Michele I need another job that's what I need. Or a Pools win. That'd be better than a kick up the arse.

Louise (*inspecting Michele's heel*) I'd put a plaster on that if I was you.

Michele Look at me, I look like a butcher's window. Bloody raw meat that. You could cook that heel, serve it up with some scraggy bit of lettuce. There's probably more goodness in my heel than there is in one of these bloody burgers.

Louise You should go to the hospital with that. I knew a girl who bled to death from her heels.

Michele Give up.

Louise I'm serious.

Michele Get away.

Louise Time is it?

Michele Twenty to.

Louise Late already.

Michele And I smell of cooking fat.

Louise You coming then or what?

Michele (*ignoring Louise*) I pong like old chips.

Louise Eh?

Michele Don't you? Niff your smock. God, it's awful. Cheap cooking fat. (*She smells herself*) Gooorr. Cheap shoes and cheap cooking fat.

Louise You should bottle that and sell it. Odour La Michele.

Michele Even my hair stinks.

Louise Could be worse.

Michele I'll have to wash this before I see Gaz.

Louise You not still seeing him tonight, are you?

Michele Yeah.

Louise When?

Michele After.

Louise It must be love.

Michele He's all right.

Louise Well it takes all sorts.

Michele Don't give me that. You said you fancied him before I went with him.

Louise I did. But there'll be nothing left of him now, will there?

Michele Cheeky sod.

Louise Not after you've had your evil way.

Michele Do you think I'm evil?

Louise Wicked.

Michele Do you?

Louise Course I do.

Michele I stink.

Louise Could be worse.

Michele So you've said.

Louise Could be on the dole.

Michele This is not much better. Our Marie nearly gets as much as I do, and she's never worked since she left school. And she's fat. Have you seen her? Fat as a pig. She's chocolate mad. Mind you I like chocolate. I could live on chocolate I could. I could, honest. Chocolate, red wine and sex.

Louise In that order?

Michele Depends on the wine.

Louise Right, that's it.

Michele Finished?

Louise Well I've done mine.

Michele Well what about mine?

Louise What about 'em?

Michele I thought you said you'd do 'em for me. If I came with you to thingy?

Louise No.

Michele That's what you said. I said I'd come if you did my tables. Fair's fair, Louise.

Louise Oh right, what did your last servant die of?

Michele Death.

Louise (*frantically tidying around, wiping tables and stacking chairs*) I thought so.

Michele Besides I can't be walking about, can I?

Louise Why?

Michele My feet are killing me.

Louise Hey, Michele, I've just remembered, I've got some chocolate in my bag.

Michele Oh brilliant. Where? (*She gets up and walks easily towards the exit*)

Louise (*starting to mop the floor*) I thought you said your feet were bad?

Michele They're not that bloody bad.

Michele exits

Music

The Lights fade to Black-out as Louise mops

SCENE 2

The judo hall

The Lights come up; the music fades

Stuart, a Black Belt in his late thirties, and Andy, also a Black Belt, who is younger and far more athletic, are limbering up. They are joined by Sarah, a younger woman who is currently a Blue Belt. The three of them clearly have known each other a long time and are very happy with their surroundings. Against the well-worn dojo, *their judo suits look worn but pristine white. A bag with Stuart's clothes in it stands to one side*

Stuart Are you sure you want to do this?
Andy Having second thoughts, are you?
Stuart Don't want to hurt you.
Andy Oh, right, that's nice of you.
Stuart Are you ready?
Andy Yes, I'm ready.
Stuart Don't say yes if you mean no.
Andy I mean yes.
Stuart I don't want you pulling your back or owt stupid.
Sarah Neither do I.
Andy I'm warm.
Stuart You should walk this championship.
Andy Come on let's make a start.
Stuart I don't want a long session.
Andy Right, let's start then.
Stuart And don't go bloody barmy wi' me — I'm putting our lass some shelves up tomorra.
Andy I won't.
Stuart I don't want to be bedridden for a bloody week.
Andy I'll take it easy.
Stuart Last time I was with you, you put me out of action for a week. Jean dun't like it.
Sarah Like that is she, Stuart?
Andy I go steady with old men, Stu.
Stuart She wants all the bloody kitchen doing. If my back goes again she'll swing for you.
Andy Right, let's start.
Sarah I'm putting the clock on for a three-minute practice.
Stuart Three minutes?
Sarah Yeh ...

Stuart Three minutes with him — he's bloody Yorkshire champion. One minute — one bloody minute. You two sods must think I've dropped off a bus.

Sarah OK. One minute *Hajime*, Stuart.

Andy is desperate to Randori. *Stuart walks around putting it off for as long as possible*

Stuart (*to Andy*) Be careful with that ankle.

Sarah You're dropping to bits, Stu.

Andy Are we getting started or what?

Stuart He's too bloody keen he is; I don't like that look he's got in his eye.

Sarah Go on, Stuart, give him what for.

Stuart He's a crafty bugger, he's strong and fast. He's the champ. You can't mess with the champ, he's too good.

Andy Stop all the "slow timing", Stuart, it won't work.

Stuart You talk through your arse, did you know that, Andy?

Andy No.

Stuart Yeh, because you've worn your mouth out.

Andy Listen who's talking.

Stuart And watch my knees, my knees are bad — no big throws. I could have been in the national squad if it wasn't for my knees.

Sarah *Hajime*, Stuart!

Andy If it wasn't for your mouth.

Sarah One minute on the clock: *Randori*. Ready?

Both Ready ...

The two men bow. Stuart grabs Andy

Sarah *Hajime*!

Stuart growls and makes a big play of the situation. He grabs Andy harder; Andy grabs him back. Stuart pulls away, shaking his wrist

Stuart Go steady with that wrist, it's weak is that.

Andy Do you mind if I hold you here? (*He holds Stuart's neck*)

Stuart No, that feels fine ...

Stuart and Andy commence Randori. *Stuart is obviously older and more cunning. Andy and Stuart continue to fight during the following*

Sarah Go on, Andy, throw him; he's only an old man.

Stuart Unfair: I'm forty-one.

Andy Don't put me off.

They try and get a better throw position

Stuart You crafty bugger.

Andy turns and throws Stuart for Ippon. *Stuart lands quite heavily and lies with his hands on his back*

Sarah Stop the clock. Thirty seconds. *Ippon* ignored. One point, or ten points. The winner: Andrew Brookes, Yorkshire champion.
Andy You all right, Stu?
Stuart Bloody hell ... I said he was crafty. I thought you were going for a big throw.
Andy You OK?
Sarah Course he is.

Sarah throws Stuart his towel

Stuart (*towelling himself down*) Look at the sweat — that's how unfit I am.
Andy I'd got you.
Stuart You'd got me before I set foot on the mat.
Andy I could have had you anytime but I thought I'd play about with you.
Stuart Don't rub it in.
Andy Are you OK?
Stuart Fell a bit heavy, that's all.

There is a pause

Yeh, it's there is that. You're good, Andy, getting very good. Yeh, good.
Andy Yeh.
Sarah Look at his head swelling.
Stuart It's true — should make the national squad this year.
Andy The Euros: that's what I want.
Stuart Well, you're good.
Sarah So you've said. Are you having another minute, Stu?
Stuart I'm having another ten minutes, then I'm off home.
Sarah *Randori?*
Stuart No, sat here. You play him — I'm cream-crackered.
Sarah OK. Three minutes ground work, how about that?
Andy I don't know if I could last three minutes on the ground with you, Sarah.
Sarah Well, you didn't do too bad last night.
Andy Tell everybody.

Sarah I'm only telling Stuart and he's past it. Ask Jean.
Stuart I will be past it if I put my back out.
Andy Don't bother about the clock, let's just fight.
Stuart Come on you two, *Hajime* ... you're worse than me.

Sarah and Andy take the middle of the stage. They face each other, fairly close together. They bow to each other, and as they do so they kiss each other on the lips

Bloody hell, get on with it.
Andy New rules, Stuart. European rules.
Stuart Tell me owt. That's what they teach you at national camp, is it? You're soft, Brookesy ...
Andy Listen what's talking.

Sarah and Andy begin to fight. Sarah attempts a number of throws on Andy but they are all aimed at the legs so he steps out of them

Andy You crafty so and so.
Stuart (*aggressively*) *Tomenage*, Sarah.
Sarah No, it's not my throw.
Stuart Whip him over, man.
Andy Don't encourage her, Stuart, it's bad enough.
Stuart Well, Brookes can't throw a Blue Belt. Wait while I tell that to the papers.

Sarah launches another attack but is thrown and held in a strangle by Andy on the floor

Nice throw!

Andy takes Sarah's arm and applies pressure to it

Go steady.
Andy Submit?
Sarah No.
Andy (*applying more pressure*) Submit?
Sarah No.
Andy Submit?
Sarah No.
Andy Come on Sarah, submit.
Sarah Never.
Andy I'll break it ...
Stuart Go steady.

Andy Submit.
Sarah Never ...
Andy Come on, submit, don't be boring.

Sarah eventually taps Andy and, relieved, he lets her go. There is a general air of relief

Good job. I could have broken it.
Sarah Wouldn't have, though.
Stuart Are we calling that it, then?
Sarah Suppose.
Stuart Yeh — have a big session on Thursday.
Sarah Where've Elaine and Gill Cotteril got to? We used to have a good session with those two.
Stuart They've left me, a'n't they? Gone up to the sports centre ... all bloody plush, new mats and all the lot. They've named it after that little fart on the council. (*He starts to get dressed*) They're all in it together up at that City Hall. You mark my words, half the judo clubs round here will end up training there. Clough's Sports Centre? I ask you. I knew that snotty bastard when I was at school.
Andy Don't mock, Stuart — they could have named it after you.
Stuart Oh, ay, I can see that right sharp.
Andy The Stuart Mason Centre.
Stuart I wouldn't swap this place for anything. Ay, they've got all the stuff, but my juniors'll beat 'em anytime. It's not a proper *dojo* that — you've got to take the mats up every time you finish.
Andy Big business, sports, these days.
Sarah When do you go back?
Andy Fortnight.
Stuart Don't forget, Andy: any chance to give us a name check, gerrit done.
Andy I do do.
Stuart I bet you do. When you're the European champion you'll not come back here.
Sarah He'd better, there's no way I'm transferring to London.

Stuart is by now fully dressed. He has a balaclava in his hand

Stuart Well, if you don't win the Nationals, I'll eat my hat.
Sarah You don't have a hat.
Stuart I'll eat my balaclava then. I'm off; I'm a bit chesty. See to everything. Are you down on Monday?
Sarah Yeh.
Stuart Right ... See you when I see you, Andy. Oh, if you see Jeff tell him

I'll be down for the juniors — there's a competition in Scunthorpe coming up. See you ...

He exits

Andy ⎫
Sarah ⎭ (*together*) See you.

A moment

Andy Do you want to do some throwing?
Sarah No ... I'm not bothered.
Andy No?
Sarah I'm tired.
Andy You'll not get a Black Belt with that attitude.
Sarah Some of us have to work, Andy.
Andy And I don't? No dedication: that's your problem.
Sarah I can't train and eat and sleep whenever I want. I work shifts.
Andy You've got a pension.
Sarah I'm not getting drawn. I'm off for a shower.
Andy Do you want a hand?
Sarah No, I think I can manage. See you in about five minutes.
Andy Five minutes. I've heard that one before.

Sarah walks off the mat, heading for the shower

Hey ...
Sarah What?
Andy Come here — we haven't finished.

Andy kneels at the side of the mat. Sarah does the same

(*Bowing*) *Owari.*
Sarah (*bowing*) *Owari* ...
Andy Right, off you go ...
Sarah That's why I want to get a Black Belt — so I can do that to you.
Andy You'll never be able to do that to me.
Sarah Oh yeh.
Andy Yes. You're not tough enough.
Sarah Right. I'm going to get the "I've had it tough" routine again, am I?
Andy (*with humour*) It's true.
Sarah I know. You were a tearaway, and your dad brought you down here to knock some sense into you, 'n' you've been here ever since. I've heard it. How old were you then. Five?

Andy Twelve.

Sarah Oh, it's changed — when I last heard it you were younger.

Andy That's very good, that is.

Sarah What did he used to sing on the way home? What was it, "A Boy Named Sue"?

Andy As good as. He was Country and Western mad. I've got most of his records. My mum saved them. He'd sit there, just watching. Seven years: every Monday, Wednesday and Saturday morning. Seven years. He never said anything, nothing, no words of encouragement, just silent, brooding, and he loved it when I was thrown about. He loved it. He'd laugh and wheeze and smoke another Woodbine. God, he loved it. But he loved it more when I started to throw the others. I think my old man was a closet sadist.

Sarah He would have been proud.

Andy Yeh. Yeh. That he would.

Sarah He wouldn't have been very proud of me looking like this.

Andy Dunno.

Sarah I wish I'd've known more about your dad.

Sarah exits to shower and change

Andy Yeh, well.

Silence

Andy is rather down, feeling sad

Louise and Michele come storming into the dojo, *wearing their* Pippins *outfits*

Andy Arrgghhhh ... Watch the mat. Shoes off.

Louise Eh? Oh God ...

Andy The mats — they're expensive.

Louise and Michele step off the mats and take their shoes off

Michele Anything else we have to take off?

Louise Sorry.

Andy Can I help you?

Michele Depends ... I hope so ...

Louise Shurrup, Michele.

Michele Well, tell him ... Before I die ...

Louise Is this the judo place?

Andy *Dojo*, yeh.
Michele You what?
Louise Shurrup, Michele.
Michele Wants a chuffin' coat of paint if you ask me.
Louise Gi' up.
Michele Well it does.
Andy What is it you want?
Louise Self-defence thingy. It wa' int' paper.
Andy Oh.
Louise Is this it?
Andy Yeh.
Michele It's her who wants it — I don't need it.
Andy No ... right.
Michele She saw it in the *Daily Mail*.
Andy It starts at six.
Louise Yeh, I know — missed bus ... (*To Michele*) I said we should have got a taxi.
Michele I wasn't gerrin a chuffin' taxi.
Louise We wa' late closing.
Andy Where?
Louise *Pippins*, in town.
Michele Do you know it?
Andy Heard of it.
Louise Can I start then?
Andy Stuart's not here. He's the fella you want for self-defence. We're doing judo.
Louise Same, i'n't it?
Andy Similar.
Louise It's taken us ages to walk from town. I'm frozen.
Michele I chuffin' am.
Andy Well, I'm not sure what to do ... Have you done any judo before?
Michele Has she chuff.
Louise Shurrup, you ... No, no, I haven't.
Andy Well, you might as well have a go; take your hat off and we'll have a go. Might as well, give you an idea. Scare you off, eh? The first thing to do is get warm. Just run around the mat — shake arms, run sideways. Get warm.

Louise starts to run around the mat

Michele (*looking on disbelievingly*) I wish I had a camera.
Andy Don't you want a go?
Michele Do I bloody hell.

Andy Right, that should do. If you've got any jewellery take it off.
Louise Right.
Michele Giz it here.

Louise removes a ring and necklace and hands them to Michele

Andy The first thing to know is that we treat the body like a ball.
Michele Ay ay.
Andy You can't be frightened of the floor. Can you forward roll?
Louise Dunno.
Andy Watch. (*He demonstrates*) Let the arm take the ground, roll across
   your shoulders, and when I go over I hit the floor with my arm to break my
   fall. Break my fall. (*He demonstrates a running break fall*) See. You have
   a good run around. Take a skip and then a forward roll. You'll have done
   this at school, very simple.
Louise Oh yeh.
Michele Go on.
Andy Go on — a skip and roll.
Louise It's just a skip and roll?
Andy Yeh.
Louise Right.
Michele Go on, that's easy — I could do it.
Louise Skip and a roll. Right. (*She runs around the* dojo. *She does a skip and
   looks as if she is about to do a roll but cries out "Arggh" and merely
   performs a sad little jump. She runs back to Andy*)

Andy smiles. Louise laughs

Michele Well that wa' chuffin' brilliant.
Louise No, I can't do it.
Andy So I see ... It looked very nice though.
Michele I'm better than that and I'm a spastic.
Louise You said it.
Andy Right let's try it on the crash mat.
Michele Oh bloody hell.

*Andy drags a large blue crash mat into the middle of the stage and stands in
front of it*

Andy Right — very simple — stand in front of it and roll over. (*He performs
   a simple roll*)
Michele It'd give me a migraine, that would.
Louise Shurrup.

Andy Have a go.
Louise Just flop over?
Andy Yeh.
Michele Watch yer knickers.

*Louise flops over on to the crash mat and is left a little ruffled but pleased —
she did it!*

Louise Oh, that's not bad ... This is comfy.
Andy To do it properly you need a suit.
Louise Right. Now I've mastered this, what next?
Andy Falling on the crash mat's easy ... you've got to learn to fall on the floor.
Louise Right ... it's just I feel a bit — frail ...
Michele Weak.
Louise Frail. I'm not a big build. It's OK if you're big, I'm not.
Andy Doesn't matter with judo, you play to your strengths.
Louise My strength is frailty.
Andy Look, let's get basic.
Michele I'm into that.
Louise (*whispering*) Will you shut it?
Michele I'm off soon.
Louise Hang on.
Andy Are you going to take this seriously?
Louise I am.
Andy You must concentrate. Lay down.
Michele Oooohhh.
Andy All you need to do is to get used to putting your hand out when you
    fall.
Louise Like this? (*She puts her arm out in the wrong place*)
Andy No ... Down the side of your body. *Ukemi* . Right? A break fall.
Louise Uk ... what?
Andy *Ukemi.*
Michele God.
Andy Watch ... very simple break fall motion.

*Andy lays on his back at Louise's side. He places his hands on his stomach
and hits each hand at the side of his body alternately*

Andy Hit the floor with force. Get a rhythm.
Michele You look pathetic.
Louise I feel it.
Michele That'd really stop a mugger, that would.
Louise Give up.

Michele I can just see you walking down your estate and this mugger or rapist saying, "Right, up against the wall" and you say, "Hang on" and you lay down and slap the bloody pavement like a drowning penguin. I'd bet he'd shit hissen.

Louise Give over.

Michele If you did that on *Top of the Pops* it'd catch on. Dance floors over the country doing that. It's be a right craze.

Louise Oh, yes I've got this, no problem. Do I get a belt for this?

Andy 'Fraid not.

Louise I could do it all day.

Michele I've never done *it* like that.

They all laugh, all enjoying the banter. The laughter continues until ...

Sarah enters. She is dressed in a police uniform and carries her shoes

The atmosphere is icy. We should get the sense that Michele and Louise and Sarah vaguely know each other

Sarah (*to Andy*) I thought we were going?

Andy Yeh, we are.

Sarah I'm ready.

Andy Yeh.

Sarah Right. Let's go.

Andy They came for Stuart's self-defence class.

Michele I didn't.

Sarah A bit late, aren't you?

Louise Missed bus.

Sarah Oh. Well, you'll have to come next time.

Louise Yeh.

Sarah When Stuart's here.

Louise I just wanted to see what it was like. I mean you never know when you might need it.

Sarah That's right.

Michele I'd just nut 'em.

Sarah That'd be good.

Michele I would, I'm not bothered.

Louise She would, her, you should see her.

Sarah I can imagine.

Louise Are you into it, then?

Sarah What?

Louise Kung fu.

Sarah It's judo.

Louise Well I know, but ...
Sarah Kung fu's different.
Louise I know, I was just joking.
Sarah Right.
Louise All part of the job for you, isn't it?
Sarah That's about it.
Louise You been doing it long?
Andy She's been doing judo for years. Blue Belt ... should be higher. She's idle.
Louise I know what you mean.
Andy What are you, Lincoln and Humberside Champion?
Louise God ... not bad.
Andy It's very good.
Louise (*to Andy*) And you're a Black Belt?
Andy Unless I'm going colour blind, yes.
Sarah Are we going, Andy?
Louise How long does it take to be a Black Belt?
Andy Depends.
Louise I bet you feel dead hard, don't you?
Andy Not really.
Sarah We said we'd lock up for Stuart.
Michele Are we off, Louise?
Louise Yeh ...
Andy Listen, if you are serious, come on Mondays, six o'clock. Stuart'll start you off. He's good. Come for a session, see what you think.
Michele Will you be here?
Andy Might be.
Sarah You'll need to buy a suit.
Louise Yeh, he said.
Andy A track suit'll do to start with.
Louise (*to Sarah*) We came straight from work.
Sarah So did I.
Michele Are we off? I'm going.

Michele exits

Louise Yeh, right ... see you ...

Louise moves to exit

Andy Hang on before you go. Stand there.
Louise What for?
Andy Bow.

Louise God, I feel daft.

They bow to each other

Andy Right, now you can go and catch your mate.
Louise See her after — I'll get off, see you.
Andy See you.
Louise Yeh, thanks a lot. Tara.
Andy Tara.
Louise (*to Sarah*) Tara ...

Sarah ignores this

  Louise leaves

There is a moment ...

Andy (*looking at Sarah*) All human life ...
Sarah Looked like you were having fun ...
Andy What a pair ...
Sarah Do you think they'll be back?
Andy You scared of the competition?
Sarah Petrified.
Andy I thought so.
Sarah I knew you'd like 'em. From the same background, aren't you?
Andy Similar.
Sarah They any good?
Andy No.
Sarah Thought as much.
Andy Know them, do you?
Sarah Know their type. Not a lot up here. (*She taps her head*)
Andy Like me then.
Sarah You said it.
Andy Well, it was a laugh.
Sarah At whose expense?
Andy Not mine, thank you.
Sarah No?
Andy Don't get so paranoid ...
Sarah You seemed to be enjoying it ——
Andy Good God, Sarah ——
Sarah It's one of those things. I don't know what you get up to when my
    back's turned ——
Andy I don't *get up* to anything.

Sarah And I'm supposed to believe that, am I?
Andy You're the detective — you tell me ...

There is a pause

Sarah Get dressed. I fancy a drink ...

Black-out

SCENE 3

Pippins. *Morning. Four days later*

The Lights come up. The seats which were stacked in the first scene are now being set by Louise and Michele. Michele is hung over

Michele I feel like death this morning.
Louise Hangover?
Michele Didn't get in till four.
Louise Where'd you go?
Michele *Peppermint's.*
Louise You ought to live there.
Michele I'll ask if I can move in.
Louise I've still got neckache. Nearly a week now, and I've still got a stiff neck.
Michele Not going back, are you?
Louise Not if I feel like this.
Michele Look at us, we're both physical wrecks.
Louise Was it good to watch?
Michele What, you flapping about?
Louise I bet it wa' brilliant.
Michelle Didn't you feel embarrassed?
Louise A bit.
Michele Only a bit? I thought you'd gone chuffin' mad.
Louise Hey, it's a laugh though.
Michele If that's what it's like every night, you're not kidding. I think I'd rather be raped than learn all that stuff.
Louise Michele.
Michele What?
Louise Don't say that.
Michele Trouble is my luck's never been in.
Louise Michele.
Michele I'm only kidding.

Louise Don't you ever get scared when you're going home?

Michele Do I chuff.

Louise I do.

Michele I don't think about it. If somebody came for me I'd frighten them to death. They'd be picking on the wrong 'un if they picked on me.

Louise You never know.

Michele About a month ago I'd just got out of a taxi up our end. And this group of lads were stood on the corner. Anyway, I walks past, and this lad says, "Hey, love, you've dropped sommat...". Anyway, I ignored 'em, and then one of 'em says, "All right, bleed to death." So I stopped. I looked round, and I just looked at 'em. They thought I was gunna run off. But I just stood there. And I stuck my finger up. (*She raises one finger*) I says "You're not worth the other one." And then I turned and walked off.

Louise Nice one.

Michele I tell you, they don't bother me.

Louise You never know though, do you?

Michele Know what?

Louise I mean, they could've got you, couldn't they?

Michele No way.

Louise I would never do that. I've wanted to. But I just keep my mouth shut and walk faster. You should see me when I get off the last bus, I'm like a tornado whizzing up our estate.

Michele (*sniffing her uniform*) I've washed this and you can still smell fat. It's even on my skin.

Louise She's supposed to be good.

Michele Who?

Louise That who-is-it. She's in the police.

Michele I'm not chuffin' thick.

Louise I wonder why she went into the police.

Michele Probably got no friends.

Louise I bet she hasn't now. I'd rather have this job.

Michele He's a bit dishy, though.

Louise I've seen him in the paper.

Michele Uhh. Superstar, eh?

Louise I knew you liked him.

Michele I was only looking.

Louise Oh, yeh. I've heard that before.

Michele Oh, I feel awful today, I might have to go home. Louise, I feel really awful.

Louise I know, I've heard you.

Michele And I've spent up.

Louise I don't suppose you fancy coming back with me, do you?

Michele Not today.

Louise We can get there early and have a mess about.

Michele I'll think about it. But I'm supposed to be seeing Gaz again on Wednesday.

Louise Oooh, right. Goodbye, Louise. Where're you going?

Michele Clubbing.

Louise *Peppermint's*?

Michele Where else?

Louise It's a toilet.

Michele No, I'm sorry. This is a toilet. You can come if you want.

Louise What, as a gooseberry?

Michele No.

Louise What then?

Michele Gaz's got this mate.

Louise Oh wonderful. I've seen Gaz's mates before, Michele. You're lucky if they can string a sentence together.

Michele They're not that bad.

Louise No, they're worse. Some of them can't even speak.

Michele I just thought it would be nice to make a foursome.

Louise Who is it? It's not Steve Little is it? 'Cos he's a dog and a half.

Michele He's all right.

Louise He's been in prison twice.

Michele Three times. Don't be such a snob. He's hard, he is, you'd be all right with him. I tell you this, nobody would pick on you if you went out with Steve Little.

Louise No wonder, is there?

Michele Why don't you come? I came with you.

Louise I came with you to meet Gaz Spencer three months ago, and I ruined my new shoes. You owe me one, Michele.

Michele (*pleading*) Oh, come. Orrr, go on.

Louise I'll think about it.

Michele Brilliant.

Louise But I'll only come if you come with me to kung fu.

Michele Judo.

Louise You know what I mean ...

Michele Right.

Louise Right what?

Michele Right. I'll think about it.

Michele makes her way off for a headache tablet

Black-out

Music

Scene 4

The dojo. *Late one evening. Some days later*

The Lights come up to reveal Stuart by himself. He is putting away various pieces of equipment and generally cleaning around. He is very proud of the dojo

The music fades

Stuart I've put everything into this. Every spare minute I've had, I've been down here, trying to make a go of it. And now they're on about closing it. What is there on this estate if they close this place? Nothing. A big, gaping nothing. We've done all sorts to keep it open. Sponsored runs, sponsored swims, sponsored walks — we even had a sponsored demolition, knocked a house down. The karate lads loved that one. They went crazy, the whole house was knocked down in a day. Mind you, it cost them dear. Sixteen broken fingers and thirty-two broken toes.

Nice little *dojo*, this. I've had some good lads and lasses come down here — well, it's safe you see. A place of refuge. Keeps them off the streets, doesn't it? And they love it. Right little sods they are when they come in, but after a month, if they stay, they're hooked. I get stuck in, no messing.

Mind you it's a funny game, this is. I've had players who'd turn out for me one month, and the next month they'd be fighting against us. Change clubs, get attracted somewhere else because they've got better mats or a new coach, or some of the national squad training there. Word gets about and "Whoosh!" — everybody's gone.

Ah, we've had some good times down here. Some right laughs, I'll tell you. I had a fella come down here about six months ago. He has a small business in town. Comes on to the mat in all the gear, looks good, nice head of hair. I remember thinking that. Thirty-five-ish, he was. He warms up, and I said, "Let's do a few break falls." So he launches himself into this break fall, and I think, "Hallo, he's done a bit, watch him." And then I see this hedgehog run across the mat — now I know it's a bit primitive down here, but a hedgehog? Anyway, this fella dives for it and sticks it on his head. It's his toupee, it's come off. Poor bloke, I couldn't do a thing for laughing. Never saw him again.

Ah, we've had some laughs.

What good is it going to do closing a place like this? I don't know.

You know some nights after training I stay behind and lock myself in. I turn the lights out, sit right in the middle of these mats and I listen to the night outside. I don't want to go home. Especially when Jean is in this mood — she's decorating mad. I just want to stay here.

Music

Stuart exits

The Lights fade to Black-out

SCENE 5

The Lights come up again on the dojo *and the music fades*

Michele, very dolled-up, enters at speed, and launches herself on to the crash mat. She screams and generally splashes about on the mat

Michele Oh ... Richard Gere ... come here ... (*She rolls about some more then gets off the mat and looks at it*) Richard, at last I've got you where I want you. You've had this coming to you for a long time, since you were in *Honorary Consul.* Get ready, Gere. (*Once again she screams and dives on to the mat*) Oooooooohhhhhhhhh! (*She "swims"*) Louise, I'm drowning, help ...

Louise (*off*) Shurruuuuup!

Michele I'm dying out here ... Hey, it'd be great to have it off on this, wouldn't it?

Louise (*off*) Shurrup ...

Michele Me and Gary Spencer on here — I can just see it. He says to me, "Moan Michele, moan; don't just lie there, moan ...". "OK, Gaz, anything you say ... I'll moan, Gaz, I'll moan ... Oooh, do you know I bring fifty-seven pounds home after tax, my mam takes twenty for my board, I've got to wash my hair, your breath smells, our Marie's pregnant, the lawn needs cutting, they're closing the ice rink, pubs shut at half-ten, and I've got to shave my legs ... How was the moaning for you, Gaz?" (*She enjoys herself with a good laugh*)

Louise enters wearing an old judogi. *The trousers are filthy; the* judogi *has paint all over it. An elastic snake belt holds the jacket closed*

Louise (*in a Chinese accent*) When you can take the pebble from my hand you are ready to leave, Glasshopper.

Michele Yes, Master ...

Louise I think he must have done the garden in this. Hey, come on, bow.

Michele stands and they bow

   Igifubmabilambadir ..
Michele Kinkyknacker oloardy.

They laugh

Louise Hey, what belt am I?
Michele Dunno.
Louise Snake belt.
Michele (*moving over to the crash mat*) Come here, it's great ...

Both girls get on to the crash mat

Louise 'S like walking on water.
Michele 'S have a wrestle.
Louise No, gi' up.
Michele (*referring to the* judogi) Where did you get this from?
Louise My Aunty Eileen dug it up for us. It used to be our Scott's.
Michele Dug it up?
Louise Yeh.
Michele It stinks.
Louise (*smelling the* judogi) I know.
Michele Strangle me ...
Louise Eh?
Michele Right, I'm a man, and I'm gonna rape you, and I don't know you're
   a self-defence expert and all that, right?
Louise Right ...

Michele dives on Louise

   Gi's a chance ...
Michele No — it wouldn't be real.
Louise Right then ...

Louise grabs Michele and they begin to wrestle on the crash mat

   *Sarah enters, wearing a track suit and looking the supreme athlete. She
   looks furiously at Michele and Louise and they stop wrestling*

Michele Hey up ...
Sarah What are you doing on that mat?
Louise Just practising.

Sarah If you're practising ground work you don't do it on the crash mat.
Louise Oh.
Sarah That mat cost this club a lot of cash.
Michele Sorry.
Sarah Yeh ... Come off it. (*To Michele*) If you are playing judo you don't
    wear ear-rings and a face full of make-up — OK?
Michele I'm not doing it.
Sarah Get off the mat then.
Michele Right.

Michele and Louise step off the mat like little kids at school

Sarah (*referring to Louise's belt*) And you'd better take that off.
Louise It's me snake belt ... It's holding my trousers up.
Sarah It's dangerous.

   Sarah exits

The two girls look at each other

Michele That, dangerous?
Louise God, yeh, it might bite me. (*She makes the snake belt bite her neck*)
Michele I'm off.
Louise Oh, wait ...

   Stuart arrives and begins to get changed

Stuart Evening.
Louise ⎫ (*together*) Evening.
Michele ⎭
Stuart Two beginners?
Louise One ...
Stuart (*to Michele*) Not you?
Michele Get chuffed.
Stuart Nice.
Louise Came last week but you'd gone.
Stuart Well, one's better than none, as I always say.
Louise Yeh.
Stuart Nice jacket.
Louise Not mine.
Stuart Take your snake belt off.
Louise It's only a joke.
Stuart Seen it.

Michele Ha ha.

Louise Well, yeh ...

Stuart What I do is, I don't mess about with falling and all that ——

Michele She's good at falling, aren't you?

Stuart What I do is give you a grounding in a bit of judo, basics. Right. First thing to do if somebody comes for you — run; run like bloody hell. The rest of it is a bit of luck. Let's say you're in a brawl, if you can get a throw in you've had a bit of luck. Right, a couple of useful throws. The first one: *Ippon Sieonage* — shoulder throw.

Louise See on what?

Stuart Bit queer i'n't it — you'll get used to it.

A pristine-looking Sarah enters and begins to warm up in the background

We're looking àt *Ippon Sieonage*.

Sarah Yeh.

Michele It's the names that gets me.

Stuart (*demonstrating*) Take hold here, with this hand. Turn your feet in, and with this hand hit them under the armpit, so that they have to come with you, see. Come towards me, striking ... I pull that and turn and you go ... Let's do it on the crash mat and then you'll get the idea ...

They move on to the crash mat. Louise leads with her left hand. Stuart grabs it, turns his body round so he is not facing her and bends forward, pulling Louise over his body

OK.

Louise Yeh, great ...

Stuart You have a go on me.

Louise tries to grab and throw Stuart but she makes a mess of it

Have another go.

Louise I can't remember it.

Stuart That arm there and that there, and turn and pull ...

Louise has another go — but is hopeless

OK ... It'll come, I'm a bit heavy for you.

Michele What if somebody eighteen stone attacks her?

Stuart This one's simple. Stand here. I push you in the chest over my blocking leg and you fall.

He demonstrates. Louise falls on the mat

You do that to me.

Louise I just step and push ...

She does the throw — not badly

Stuart Do it again ...

Louise throws Stuart again

That's good. It's just a simple step and push and over they go.
Michele What do you do then?
Stuart Run.
Michele Karate's better than judo.
Stuart In a game of judo — come here — I'd throw you, and then I'd hold
you down ...
Louise Oh ...
Stuart That's how I'd win. Watch. Right. (*He throws her while saying the
following*) ... *Osoto gari* and then, on the floor, I'd hold you; there are all
different holds. And I've won.
Louise So judo's a game?
Stuart Olympic sport, yeh.
Louise God ...
Stuart You try *Osoto gari* on me. No, tell you what — try it on Sarah.
Sarah ... *Osoto gari* ... let her try it.

Sarah comes over. Louise holds her

Sarah Get a good hold — that's too weak.

Sarah grabs Louise's arm. Louise grabs Sarah's judogi *but her grip is not
strong enough so her hand comes away*

Hold strong, like this, and when you come in, come in strong.

Sarah holds Louise and demonstrates the hold to her, holding her very hard

Louise Bloody hell.
Stuart (*to Louise*) She's technically better than me, actually. (*To Sarah*)
Throw her and hold her, give a sense of what it's like. On the mat, then a
hold.
Louise Don't hurt me.
Sarah No.
Louise (*to Michele*) Arrrhhh.
Sarah Just stand there ...

Sarah launches Ippon Sieonage — *and Louise crashes on to the mat. Sarah goes for a stranglehold and puts Louise under some pressure. Louise tries to struggle but cannot escape so she pulls Sarah's hair, which makes Sarah all the more determined to keep the hold on. Louise screams*

Michele Hey, you can't do that, can you?
Stuart Yeh.
Michele Bloody hell.
Stuart Tap ... tap her arm ...

Louise taps Sarah's arm; Sarah releases her

Louise Good God ...
Sarah Don't pull hair. If you want to submit, tap.
Louise Now you tell me.
Sarah Just tap, right?
Michele Nice one, Louise, nearly pulled her chuffin' hair out.
Louise What d'you expect?
Michele (*to Louise, half-sincere*) All right?
Louise Couldn't breathe.
Sarah That's the idea.

Sarah exits

Stuart She's OK — aren't you?
Louise Dunno. I thought it was going to be all nice and gentle. She frightened me to death.
Stuart Once you get used to it, you'll be laughing.
Michele I don't think I would.
Louise (*holding her neck*) Oh, my neck; I'm burning.
Michele It's too rough if you ask me. Somebody could get hurt. You'd be better off buying a pellet gun, I think.
Stuart As soon as you tap, your opponent releases.
Louise You could have told me.
Stuart Yeh, sorry, sometimes I forget all the basic stuff.
Louise Oh, great.
Stuart You're all right, aren't you?
Louise I liked that bit best, on that mat.
Stuart That's just for beginners.
Louise I thought I was a beginner.

Sarah enters with a towel around her neck

Stuart No, you look tougher than that, don't you reckon, Sarah?

Sarah What's that?

Stuart These two look tough nuts.

Sarah Oh yeh, yeh.

Michele How long have you been doing it, then?

Stuart Too long. Since I can remember, really. You know some of the top Japanese are like you, they don't know when to submit. You can have them in an arm lock, breaking their arm, and they won't give in. That's when it becomes a war of nerves. Should you break their arm or should you ease off a bit? And as soon as you ease off, "Bang!" they turn it against you, and they've got you.

Sarah You're not like that though, are you, Stuart?

Stuart I'm not. As soon as you've nearly got the lock on me, I'm tapping like blue murder.

Michele Where's who-is-it?

Stuart What?

Michele That other bloke?

Sarah Andy?

Michele Yeh.

Stuart Fighting this week. Holland, isn't it?

Sarah That way, yeh.

Michele Doesn't he come any more?

Sarah When he can.

Michele Right.

Sarah Why?

Michele Is he any good?

Sarah Very good.

Michele Didn't look all that good last time, did he Louise?

Sarah He's very good actually. He's with the national squad.

Michele Him and her were just laid on the floor flapping about.

Louise He was just having a laugh, that's all.

Michele Oh yeh? I've heard that before.

Louise It was just a laugh.

Michele I thought you said you fancied him?

Louise No. I never said that.

Michele You did, you liar.

Louise I don't.

Michele I thought you said you did?

Louise No.

Michele Oh, well, I do, I think he's all right.

Louise Anyway. We haven't come for that, have we?

Stuart (*intervening in this delicate area*) So are you two going to stay and do something with us or is that about enough for one night? (*To Michele*) What about you, d'you want to train with us?

Michele You what?

Stuart Do you want to train with me and Sarah?

Michele Get stuffed. You must be off your perch.

Stuart Such a lovely girl.

Louise We'd better go. I've had enough for a start.

Stuart Sure?

Louise Absolutely certain. Can't move my neck.

Stuart Right. See you Wednesday, will I?

Michele (*to Louise*) You're not coming again, are you? It's stupid. Why come again? They will break your neck next time.

Louise and Michele begin to move away from the mat. During the following dialogue they exit

Louise Why don't you shut your gob?

Michele I'm not coming again, it's a bloody nightmare. Are we going to get a drink? I'm gagging. Hey, Stu thingy, you know that there's no clean water in there, don't you? I tried to get a drink but it comes out black. Thought it was coffee or something.

They are gone

Sarah and Stuart look at each other. Silence

Stuart Right, WPC, are you ready?

Sarah Just about.

Stuart When is he back?

Sarah Weekend, I think.

Stuart How's it been going?

Sarah I haven't heard. I don't even know if they've got there. Could be lost at sea. You know what Andy's like — when he's away from home he forgets how to use a telephone.

Stuart Probably busy.

Sarah It's the same every time, Stuart. When he's with the squad nothing else exists.

Stuart It's got to be like that. Total commitment.

Sarah He's probably taking in the sights of Old Amsterdam.

Stuart He can't be thinking about back home when there's some strutting great Swede threatening to break your neck.

Sarah The difference is, I would.

Stuart You don't go away.

Sarah I wish I did.

Stuart They'll be having a great time.

Sarah That's what I'm afraid of. Will he come back in one piece?

Stuart About ten years ago I went to Düsseldorf. That was before my knees gave way. What a laugh. It was a European Open, invitation thing, you know, like a demonstration, before it all got serious. They put us up in this big city hotel. There were about ten of us. Six blokes, four women. I didn't tell Jean. I daren't. She'd've stopped me from going. We had no drinks before, but we made up for it after. I think they were happy to see the back of us. Four o'clock one morning, Pete McKenzie was streaking through the hotel foyer, completely out of his head. We came down to watch him. Somebody had called the police. They dragged him screaming and bollock naked into a police car. Talk about laugh — we were all killing ourselves.

Sarah Yeh, that's my point. Total commitment, eh Stu?

Stuart That's right. Total commitment.

Sarah Yeh?

Stuart When you work as hard as Andy does, Sarah, you've got to expect him to play hard as well.

Sarah Oh right. Thanks. I didn't realize.

Sarah makes her way off the mat towards the exit

Stuart Where're you going?

Sarah For a run: commitment, remember?

Stuart I thought we were supposed to be training?

Black-out

Music

SCENE 6

The dojo. *The following week*

The Lights come up and the music fades

Michele and Louise enter in their Pippins *clothes. They take off their shoes*

Michele Let's go on the big mat.

Louise No.

Michele Why?

Louise 'Cos I wanna learn don't I?

Michele 'S boring ...

Louise If you want to learn you've got to practise. Andy trains all day.

Michele It's his job — he gets paid for it.

Louise Sponsored.

Michele Same.

Louise He's in the national finals at the end of this month.

Michele You're barmy on him.

Louise If he wins, think what it'll do for t' area. And I'm not barmy on him, actually.

Michele It won't do owt 'cos nobody's bothered.

Louise Oh, it would Michele, nobody ever does anything from round here. It's brilliant.

Michele He's just another big head.

Louise Take your tights off.

Michele Hey, you kinky bitch.

Louise Take 'em off.

Michele What for?

Louise *Uchi* ...

Michele *Uchi* bloody what?

Louise Practise ... throwing ...

Michele What's my tights got to do with it?

Louise You'll see; tek 'em off.

Michele takes off her tights during the following

Michele I thought you'd've got fed up of this fad by now. Three months you've been doing it. I think you're going chuffing light, me, if you ask me — so does everybody at work. Here (*she hands Louise the tights*) they'll not fit you.

Louise I'm not going to wear 'em. Here, hold that ... (*the pantie part of the tights*) ... I'm gonna practise some throwing.

Michele Watch me tights ...

Louise Shurrup and stand still.

Michele I think I'm dafter than you.

Louise Hold 'em tight.

Michele I am.

Louise holds the feet of the tights and begins to step in for a sequence of throws. This is the equivalent of shadow boxing; she uses the tights to go through the arm and foot movements of a Tiaotoshi

Louise Open your legs ...

Michele Are you going kinky?

Louise Shurrup. (*She begins to turn into different throws*)*Tiaotoshi*. (*She turns in for* Tiaotoshi)

Michele This is really great, this. What do you do in your dinner hour, Michele? Oh, I take my tights off and let Louise ladder 'em.

Louise *Sieonage ... Tiaotoshi ...*

Michele There was a riot at *Peppermint's* on Friday.

Louise *Tiaotoshi ...*

Michele Cops all over the place in town. Twenty arrested.

Louise *Sieonage.*

Michele Pity you weren't there, could have sorted 'em all out ...

Louise Funny.

Michele Gaz was involved. Got glassed — he's not bothered.

Louise *Ippon sieonage ...*

Michele Seven stitches about his eye. Looks great — too hard.

Louise *Tiaotoshi.*

Michele Look at me tights — I've got to wear these.

Louise Will you stand still?

Michele Will I chuff ...

Louise Come on, what's up?

Michele I'm fed up, that's what's up. Fed up of you and this pigging stuff. It's boring: *Osh* this, bloody *Ohishit* that — you're a bore; you're gerring like a chuffin' fella.

Louise What you on about?

Michele You.

Louise What?

Michele You piss me off.

Louise How come?

Michele I'm not interested in it, OK? Do you think I like doing this every dinner break?

Louise 'S only once a week.

Michele So what — it's boredom. I'm not interested in the European fights, or this and that, OK?

Louise Listen, Michele, I'm not that interested in how many were killed at *Peppermint's* or how many times you and Gaz do it a night or how many stitches he's got.

Michele Well, you ought to be, 'cos that's the real world, not this.

Louise Put your brain in before you talk, Michele.

Michele Right. What are you doing this for?

Louise A laugh.

Michele It i'n't funny.

Louise Oh, piss off, Michele.

Michele I will.

Louise Go on, then.

Michele I will!

Louise Well, go then, I'm not scared of you.

Michele You think you're rock ——

Louise I don't.

Michele I'll crack you in a minute.

Louise Oh yeh.

Michele Yeh ...

Louise You couldn't crack a joke.

Michele Funny ...

Louise Yeh ...

Michele You think you're fucking it.

Louise I don't.

Michele What are you trying to be sommat that you're not for — who are you trying to impress, eh?

Louise I'm not trying to impress you.

Michele Gi's me tights ...

Louise (*handing them over*) Here, have 'em.

Michele Look at 'em.

Louise You'll not need to put them on if you're going to see Gaz, will you?

Michele Go and die.

Louise And you.

Michele You're a freak. That's what everyone says at work. Must be something wrong with her. A grown woman taking up judo.

Louise Sommat to do.

Michele I'd rather watch paint dry.

Louise Yeh, that's about all you're good for.

Michele You what?

Louise You heard.

Michele What did you say?

Louise I said it's about all you're good for ...

Michele (*moving near to Louise, threateningly, then grabbing her aggressively*) I'll drop you in a minute you little cow.

Louise Get off.

Michele Or what?

Louise Get off.

Michele Are you saying I'm thick?

Louise No.

Michele You are.

Louise I'm not.

Michele You are.

Louise Get off.

Michele (*grabbing Louise and pinning her to the floor*) I thought you were supposed to be good?

Louise Get off.

Michele I thought you were supposed to be good, Louise?

Louise Get off.

Michele You think you're it, don't you? Well, I'm not scared of you, Underwood, so don't think I am. All right?

Louise Yeh.
Michele All right?
Louise Yeh. Yeh.
Michele I'm not fucking scared of you. (*She spits a large gob into Louise's face*)

Black-out

Music

SCENE 7

The dojo

The Lights come up and the music fades

Sports bags adorn the side of the mat

Andy has Stuart in a hold on the floor. Stuart is desperately trying to get out of the hold

Andy Struggle.
Stuart I am struggling.
Andy Can't feel it.
Stuart Andy, I'm definitely struggling.
Andy This is when he tried to turn me — strong fella he was, Stu ——
Stuart Ray Collins?
Andy No, Dobson, in the final — very strong ——
Stuart Watch my arm.
Andy I had to grip and hold on; God, I was pulling for grim death.
Stuart You're — er — breaking my arm, Andy ...
Andy There I was — didn't think he'd submit.
Stuart You're definitely breaking my arm, Brookesy.
Andy And then he tapped — submission ...
Stuart (*tapping Andy*) I'm tapping, I'm bloody well tapping.

Andy releases Stuart

Couldn't you feel me tapping?
Andy I was miles away.
Stuart I was nearly miles away, in the bloody hospital.

Sarah, wearing a Brown Belt, enters carrying a trophy and medal

Sarah Oh, we're not having the "How I Won the War" story again are we?

Andy I was just showing Stuart.

Sarah How boring.

Stuart He's nearly done my arm in.

Andy Sorry, mate ...

Sarah I've been through that nearly a dozen times.

Andy Well ... I mean ——

Stuart I think it's terrific. I do.

Sarah He's done well.

Andy Are we having a run before we start?

Stuart I thought we'd get started.

Andy No, have a jog.

Stuart I tell you something, Andy, you want to have a word with this one here.

Andy Sarah?

Stuart She comes for a week or two and then lapses, and comes back when you're here.

Sarah I've been busy.

Andy Juliet Bravo?

Sarah Don't start.

Stuart Well, I think it's tremendous, national and European champion — from *this* club, smallest in Hull. Good God, I'd like to see the look on their faces up at sports centre.

Andy Are they still on about knocking this place on the head?

Stuart Dunno ... maybe.

Andy (*looking at Sarah's belt*) Hang on, do I detect a change in colour here?

Sarah Ha ha — my little surprise.

Andy I should have thought to ask ...

Sarah Yeh, you should, but I'll try to forgive you. If you behave yourself.

Andy Suits you.

Sarah Thanks ... I'm quite pleased with it myself, actually.

Andy I bet you are.

Stuart Black next.

Sarah Hope so.

Andy It gets tougher ——

Sarah So I understand.

Andy We'd better watch ourselves now, Stu.

Stuart Yeh.

Andy Oh, no, next month I'm in a civic "It's a Knockout" for Hull. I've got tickets, you'll have to come.

Stuart Where is it?

Andy Scunthorpe.

Sarah Hitting the big time.

Stuart From Holland to Scunthorpe — now that's what I call cosmopolitan.
Sarah (*musing*) Sunny Scunny ...
Andy Yeh, if Typhoo put the "T" in Britain, who put the ——
Stuart Heard it.
Sarah I haven't.
Stuart You wouldn't get it ...
Sarah (*sarcastically*) I live a very sheltered existence.

Louise enters the dojo *with her sports bag and takes off her track suit during the following. She has her* judogi *on underneath — with a Yellow Belt*

Stuart Late?
Louise Yeh, sorry. My mum's ill at the moment, my dad's having a panic, and I had to do the supermarket.
Andy Still at it are you?
Louise Still trying. Oh, er — well done ...
Andy Thanks ...
Louise (*kissing Andy on the cheek*) Saw you on *Grandstand* ...
Andy I wasn't on for long. Blink and you'd missed me.
Louise Yeh, that's what I thought. I waited all afternoon for it to come on, then suddenly, flash, ten seconds of judo and then back to the horse racing. Desperate, that is. Hey, my mum saw you on breakfast telly an' all. That's all she does these days, she's glued to the box.
Andy I'm doing an "It's a Knockout" thingy, want to come?
Louise Me ... ?
Stuart Bring your mate ——
Louise She doesn't work with me any more.
Andy Oh ...
Louise (*seeing the trophy*) Good trophy.
Andy Yeh.
Louise Brilliant. Have you given it to your mum?
Andy Eh?
Louise If I won one I'd give it to my mum — for the mantelpiece.
Stuart Wait till you've got one.

Everyone shares a laugh at Louise's expense

Sarah Some wait.
Stuart Hey, she's coming on — a natural left-handed *Tiaotoshi*, aren't you?
Louise Am I?
Stuart Yeh.
Andy Show us, then.

Louise No.
Andy Come on ...
Louise No — I feel dead shown up.
Andy When are you going for your Green Belt?
Louise About nineteen ninety-eight.
Stuart Next gradings.
Louise I've got a licence.
Andy Great. (*He becomes dismissive towards Louise; to Stuart*) Are we
   jogging?
Stuart Can do ...

Stuart and Andy put on their track suits and other jogging gear during the
following

   You coming, Sarah?
Sarah No.
Andy Right, ten minutes, and then we'll come back and I'll throw you about,
   Stuart.
Stuart Take it steady, Brookesy ...
Andy We haven't started yet.
Stuart I know.
Andy A good run'll get your blood flowing.
Stuart It'll also knacker my knees up.
Andy Come on ...

Stuart and Andy leave

Sarah }
Louise } (*together*) See you ...

There is an awkward atmosphere in the dojo *now; Louise cannot face Sarah*

Louise He's done brilliant, a'n't he?
Sarah Yes.
Louise Brilliant — for the club and that ...
Sarah Yes, very good.
Louise He's a good player — i'n't he?
Sarah He ought to be, it's his life.
Louise I know; I mean, I bet it must have to be.

There is another pause. They begin to move and get warm, stretch and the like

Sarah Do you want to have a session?

Louise Who?

Sarah There's only you here.

Louise Oh yeh, right ... er, er — yeh. Can do. I'm still a bit — awkward.

Sarah Raw?

Louise Well, yeh. I thought you'd stopped coming. Haven't seen you for ages.

Sarah Been doing my study, that and working nights.

Louise Been a lot of trouble a'n't there, at *Peppermint's*?

Sarah It's the same every Friday.

Louise Congratulations.

Sarah What for?

Louise points to Sarah's belt

Oh, this ... yes.

Louise It's very good — Brown Belt.

Sarah Yeh.

There is a moment's pause

Louise You don't like me, do you?

Sarah What is there about you to like?

Louise I've never offended you, have I?

Sarah Just keep your eyes off Andy.

Louise That's stupid, I've never even ... oh, don't be daft — that's daft, honest.

Sarah Well as long as we know where we stand. You ready?

Louise Yeh. Go easy with me.

Sarah (*bowing*) *Rei* ...

Louise (*bowing*) *Rei* ...

The two girls grab each other. Sarah throws Louise and gets her on the floor straight into an arm hold. Louise taps Sarah; Sarah releases her

That's really good.

Sarah You aren't trying, are you?

Louise I am, yeh ...

Sarah Again. (*She bows*) *Rei* ...

Louise (*bowing*) *Rei*.

Again the two girls fight. Sarah throws Louise and once again catches her easily in a pin. Sarah keeps Louise pinned down

Sarah You've got to fight back.
Louise I am ...
Sarah If you don't fight back I'm going to hurt you.

They both get to their feet

Louise Look, I'm not too good at this: can't we do something else?
Sarah This is how you get good — *Randori.*
Louise I'm going, Sarah.
Sarah You're not ——
Louise I'm going to go ——
Sarah You're stopping here and training. (*She grabs Louise*)
Louise Will you let go, please?
Sarah No.
Louise Please.
Sarah What're you going to do about it?
Louise Why are you doing this?
Sarah Doing what? I only want a decent fight. Come on, fight me.
Louise You're hurting me.

Their voices rise to a crescendo during the following

Sarah Come on, fight.
Louise No.
Sarah Fight.
Louise No.
Sarah Let's see how good you are ...
Louise No.
Sarah Yes.
Louise I don't want to.
Sarah Come on ...

Louise starts to fight with Sarah. It is a hard fight, with them both wrestling for position. Louise, fuming, tries to throw Sarah. She can't; Sarah is too canny. Sarah throws Louise and gets her in a pin on the floor

Louise (*tapping submission*) You're hurting me ...
Sarah Am I?
Louise (*still tapping*) Sarah — you're suffocating me ...

Andy enters, out of breath from running. He takes in the scene

Andy Sarah ...?

Louise taps again

Sarah!

Sarah lets go and gets up. Louise remains on the ground in tears

Andy Looked a bit serious.
Sarah No ...
Andy She's only a Yellow Belt.
Sarah She wanted to play rough, that's all. You know what they're like,
 Andy.
Andy She's only a little player.
Sarah (*getting up and taking the trophy*) I'll keep this safe, Andy. You never
 know, things do go missing ...

Sarah exits to the dressing rooms

Andy You all right?
Louise No.
Andy Tough at the bottom, eh?
Louise She made me fight her ...
Andy Come on — you'll take a lot worse if you're going to keep at it ...
Louise I'm not — I'm not coming any more.
Andy Because of that?
Louise No.
Andy What then?

*Louise takes off her belt and throws it at Andy. During the following she
stands and walks towards the exit from the* dojo

Louise Here, have that.
Andy Don't be stupid, we all take knocks ——
Louise No, that's it, finished. I should have listened to Michele — she said
 I was stupid, and I am.
Andy You're having a go, aren't you?
Louise Why? Why am I? I must be off my perch. What a bloody joke. I've
 packed my best mate in for this. I must be a bloody lunatic. (*She kicks the
 crash mat, in a fit of temper*) I'm off, I've had enough.

There is a beat of silence

*Louise has really hurt her foot. She holds it and falls on to her back on the
crash mat. As she does she mouths, without noise, "Fucking hell"*

A quick Black-out

Music

Curtain

ACT II

SCENE 1

The Pippins *set has been struck; the higher level is now completely empty*

The dojo. *Some time later*

The interval music continues under the beginning of the scene

It is calm in the dojo, *in contrast to the violence of the outside world*

Louise enters, bringing with her a large cassette player; the music now comes from this. She wears judo bottoms and a T-shirt. She is about to commence a big training session and will not want to be disturbed. She warms up by stretching to the music. She bends and turns, stretches and twists. Her movements are very graceful, almost balletic. She should give the impression of being well-advanced in the process of becoming an athlete, very sexy and almost a different person from the Louise of ACT I. *There is a confidence in her stance and poise and she is sure-footed rather than clumsy. She takes a few dumb-bells and slowly exercises to the music. After this, she jogs and shakes out. She looks like a panther, clearly "going places" in the sport*

Michele enters, looking tarty in a miniskirt and make-up. She watches Louise, standing on the edge of the mat

Michele Hey up ...?
Louise (*stopping her exercises and looking at Michele*) All right?
Michele I thought I'd find you here.
Louise (*switching off the cassette player*) Yeh.
Michele I ... erm ... well.
Louise What?
Michele I've been up your end ...
Louise Yeh?
Michele Nobody in.
Louise Yeh. Flitted, a'n't you?
Michele Yeh.
Louise Denise told me at work.
Michele Live up Sutton Park.

Louise Nice.
Michele How's *Pippins*?
Louise Crap.
Michele I'm ... er ... working in the *Pecan*.
Louise Italian?
Michele Yeh — sexy blokes ... (*She laughs*)
Louise (*uninterested*) Yeh.
Michele Yeh.

A pause

How's the judo thingy?
Louise All right.
Michele Got a Blue Belt?
Louise Blue, yeh.
Michele 'S'good, i'n't it?
Louise All right for the time being.

Silence

Michele Me and Gaz have split ...
Louise Oh.
Michele About four months ago — at *Peppermint Park* — I just thought I'd
    tell you.
Louise Oh.
Michele I'm seeing Steve.
Louise Little?
Michele Yeh.
Louise God — getting about a bit, aren't you?
Michele You know me.

Silence

They're closing this place, aren't they?
Louise Maybe ...
Michele I saw it in t' paper.
Louise We're making an appeal.
Michele Does dishy Andy still come?
Louise Not very often — trains in London.
Michele Is he still seeing who-is-it?
Louise Yeh.

A pause

Michele Cold in here.
Louise I'm quite warm.
Michele It's freezing.
Louise It's warm if you train.
Michele Yeh, I suppose it would be.
Louise Keeps me weight down.
Michele You look slimmer.

Silence

Louise Going somewhere?
Michele I was doing.
Louise *Peppermint's*?
Michele No ...
Louise Oh.
Michele Nowhere, really.
Louise Oh.
Michele I thought that you might want to come.
Louise You've just said you're not going anywhere.
Michele Well, for a drink.
Louise Well.
Michele I thought it'd be nice to have a night out ... like we used to.
Louise I'm not bothered any more, Michele.
Michele About going out?
Louise We've had some good laughs, but ... look at me ... can't you see that I've found sommat?
Michele You said some horrible things to me.
Louise You said some horrible things behind my back.
Michele I didn't.
Louise You did, because Denise told me.
Michele Well, come for a talk then.

Louise gives Michele a look

Louise Look at yourself, 'Chel ...
Michele What?
Louise You look cheap.
Michele I do not.
Louise You do.
Michele And you're a chuffin' saint, aren't you?
Louise I don't go about looking like a bag.
Michele What're you trying to prove, Louise?
Louise What do you mean?

Michele I know you can fight me so what are you trying to prove?

Louise I'm not trying to prove anything.

Michele So why all this kung fu stuff?

Louise Why? Because I got fed up.

Michele Fed up of what? We had a great laugh.

Louise I got fed up spending every night in the *Bass House*, waiting for some bloke to throw me the odd line, fed up hanging around the *Shire Horse* looking like I'd just stepped out of a bloody catalogue, waiting to have some slobbering bloke ask to take me home ... You're trying to prove sommat, dressed like that. I'm not trying to prove anything, I'm doing it. If you wanna continue gerrin' felt up behind the gents' toilets or stealing a sly shag in the bus station, that's fine by me.

Michele I don't get felt up ...

Louise Tough luck.

Michele I came here in all good faith, Louise, not to get the chuffin' earache.

Louise I didn't ask you to come.

Michele I thought we were friends?

Louise We were.

Michele Oh, chuff off then.

Louise Listen Michele, I'm not falling out with you; I'm just saying I've changed.

Michele I have ...

Louise Have you?

Michele I want sommat an' all, Louise — I chuffing well want sommat ...

Louise Well, do sommat about it, then.

Michele How can I?

Louise You don't have to go out every night.

Michele Don't I?

Louise No.

Michele What am I supposed to do? Sit in our house, listen to my mam and dad shout it out? I'd chuffin' suffocate listening to that lot. It comes in on me. I can't stop in — I've got to go out.

Louise But look at yer ...

Michele Look at you: your life's going and you're throwing it away ——

Louise That's exactly what I'm *not* doing.

Michele Who the fuck do you think you are? You're just like me, you know, you're nobody special.

Louise Don't start, Michele.

Michele Yeh.

Louise Don't start.

Michele I hate you. Hear that, Underwood, I chuffin' hate you.

Louise Come and do something about it then.

Michele Funny.

Louise It is, isn't it? Funny gobbin' in people's faces, isn't it? Come on then,
   you shag bag, come and do something about it.
Michele I hate you.
Louise Look, Michele, why don't you just go and get shagged.

There is a pause

Michele Don't worry, I will do.

Black-out

Music

SCENE 2

The dojo

The Lights come up; the music fades

*The crash mat is in the corner of the room with Andy and Sarah reclined on
it. Andy has a bandaged foot. They are very close and intimate, pecking and
fondling throughout much of the early dialogue*

Sarah Andy?
Andy What?
Sarah Can I ask you something?
Andy Depends ...
Sarah (*having second thoughts*) No, it's not important.
Andy Go on.
Sarah No.
Andy Go on.
Sarah No, it doesn't matter,
Andy Oh great — now I'm wondering ...
Sarah I'll feel embarrassed ...
Andy Embarrassed?

A moment

Sarah Have you ever been with anyone else, you know, since you've been
   with me?
Andy No.
Sarah Sure?
Andy I should know.

Sarah Oh.
Andy Why?
Sarah Oh nothing — I thought, maybe ...
Andy When?
Sarah Holland ...
Andy No way ...
Sarah Oh ...

A moment

Andy What about you?
Sarah Me?
Andy Yeh, you.
Sarah Nooooo.
Andy What about all the strange men you go out with at nights — who's that copper? Tony ... Weston ...
Sarah Tony Simpson.
Andy Tony Simpson — what about him?
Sarah Spare me. Spotty Simpson — he's a joke.
Andy But you're out with him every night — I feel jealous.
Sarah In a Panda car.
Andy Women in uniforms — it does strange things to a man.
Sarah Someone has already done "strange things" to Tony Simpson.
Andy Really?
Sarah Yes — really.
Andy What happened on Friday?
Sarah Night?
Andy When else?
Sarah A bit of a scene at *Peppermint's* ...
Andy Sounded like a grand opera.
Sarah A bus full of stags from Doncaster, on a stag night — very nasty ...
Andy Don't you get frightened?
Sarah Yeh. All the time. Drunks, down and outs, unmarked cars, you name it. Scares me shitless. There was a young lad on Friday needed thirty-seven stitches in his face.
Andy Thirty-seven. Jesus.
Sarah Somebody glassed him because he was from out of town.
Andy They ought to lynch 'em.
Sarah Got to catch them first. He wasn't doing anything wrong either. I suppose he just looked different.
Andy I don't go out into town any more. It's like bedlam.
Sarah At least you can look after yourself. This poor kid was about five foot two and seven stone, wet through.

Andy So, are you training tonight, or what?

Sarah Every weekend it's the same.

Andy So let's see some action.

Sarah Oh, right, Master.

Andy Thank you, that's the respect I deserve.

Sarah Did you know that seven minutes' passionate love-making is equivalent in calorie loss to a three-mile run?

Andy Get away.

Sarah True.

Andy Where did you hear that?

Sarah It's true.

Stuart And I've been running thirty miles a week for the last ten years?

Sarah You learn something new every day.

Andy So they say. (*Pause*) So you aren't training?

Sarah Later.

Andy Later never comes.

Sarah I want to talk. Ask you some advice.

Andy You want advice from me; are you well?

Sarah I've been offered a job at Clough's. Two nights a week. Obviously when I can fit it in. Fifteen quid a night.

Andy What is it?

Sarah Well, it's a bit of self-defence and women's keep fit.

Andy Self-defence? You'll end up like Stuart.

Sarah And keep fit.

Andy Right.

Sarah A fella at work does a karate class up there. They've got Carole Green doing a class. She's a kendo expert.

Andy That'll be useful; you'll have to walk about with a big stick.

Sarah Brian Cooke asked me if I fancied doing a bit. You know, basic stuff.

Andy Oh, right. I get it, just "Kick 'em in the balls". Is that it? That'll make a difference? Keep away from dark alleys. Don't fight, run. Keep away from drunks with broken glasses.

Sarah Thirty quid a week. Better than a poke in the eye.

Andy I don't think it is.

Sarah Are you joking?

Andy Do you think it'll make any difference? Twice a week for an hour at a time. You'll be lucky if you get the same women coming back more than once. It's a fad. A little knowledge is dangerous.

Sarah So what would you rather we do, not have any classes at all? That'd be good. Very reassuring. I can't believe you're saying this.

Andy I've spent my life doing this. Once a week touching your toes won't make any difference.

Sarah I think it will.

Andy No way.

Sarah We won't be touching our toes.

Andy Sarah, if you give anybody the faintest idea that they might stand a chance, you're actually doing them a massive disservice. You know that. It takes years. Years. What would you do if somebody came for you?

Sarah Run.

Andy Right, and so would I. It's not a game, nobody's going to tap submission and shake hands.

Sarah I know that, but I think it can make a difference.

Andy Do you?

Sarah Don't you?

Andy Not enough difference, that's my point.

Sarah Well, I've already told them I'm doing it.

Andy So you didn't want my advice; all you wanted was my approval?

Sarah I actually believe it's worth the effort. Some people aren't even aware of the danger.

Andy I do know that. All I'm saying is, it's a way of life, not a flaming relaxation technique. It's not like an art class night school. You don't just throw a pot one week, and then go on to water colours.

Sarah I am aware of all this. I have given it some thought. Or does that surprise you?

Andy When do you start?

Sarah Next week.

Andy So you're deserting poor old Stu?

Sarah Oh what? Don't give me that. There's nothing happening down here any more, you said that yourself. Stuart knows this place is going to close. All that stuff in the paper was just Stuart's way of bowing out in style. I mean, look at it.

Andy What did they teach you at police college, Sarah?

Sarah Don't start that.

Andy Whatever happened to the Community Constable?

Sarah can't respond

Louise enters. As usual, she is hurriedly arriving from Pippins wearing her work clothes; she carries her sports bag

Sarah Ah, here she is, the next Karen Briggs.

Andy Praise indeed.

Louise You know you are in grave danger of being amusing, did you know that?

Andy Touché.

Sarah It was a compliment.

Louise Hi, Andy.
Andy Hi.
Louise Bad foot?
Andy "It's a Knockout."
Louise Certainly was. Where's Stuart ...?
Andy Probably decorating.
Louise Oh ... I'll get changed then.

Louise exits to the changing rooms

Sarah She's Stuart's protégée now, is she?
Andy Now, now, you were once.
Sarah Was I that awkward, though?
Andy She's OK ...
Sarah Andy?
Andy Sorry, she's foul — but she is determined.
Sarah She's OK.
Andy I see she's ditched her mate.
Sarah I don't like her. She's too deep. You know what I mean, she looks a
  bit devious.
Andy Oh yeh, very devious.
Sarah Well, she does.
Andy Does she hell.
Sarah It's a woman's thing.
Andy Is it?
Sarah It is.
Andy It's jealousy.
Sarah Jealousy — are you joking?
Andy No.
Sarah Me?
Andy She's come through her grades very quickly.
Sarah She'll never make a Black Belt.
Andy I wouldn't be so sure.
Sarah Never.
Andy She's a good player ...
Sarah She's *(with emphasis)* OK.

Louise enters wearing her kit, with a Blue Belt, and begins to warm up

Andy Did you ever get a new suit?
Louise No — I keep this. It was our Scott's — bring me luck.
Sarah What belt was "our Scott"?
Louise Snake belt, I think.

Sarah Thought as much.

Louise No hang on, I think he was a Leather Belt, but he could have been a First Dan pair of braces, or a Black Belt jock strap.

Sarah (*deliberately*) Ha ha.

Louise Doesn't matter what belt: when you win, enjoy it for one day but no more.

Sarah Says who?

Louise Kashiwazaki — the God of Judo.

Andy Very impressive. You read all that stuff now, do you?

Louise Right, are we training, or what?

Andy I can't — my foot: Kashiwazaki say, he with bad foot cannot do judo.

Louise Sarah?

Sarah No, I've got a competition coming up ...

Louise So? I've got a grading next month.

Sarah I need some decent opposition.

Louise Let's just throw in that case.

Sarah Throw a Blue Belt ... no, I don't think I'll bother.

Louise Come on, you throw me, I'll throw you.

Sarah I don't think you'll throw me.

Louise You're easy.

Andy That's fighting talk.

Sarah No way.

Louise Come on ...

Sarah No way.

Louise What's a matter, frightened are you?

Sarah Listen to the worm turning.

Louise Let's get sommat done.

Andy Just do some throwing, the both of you.

Sarah I don't know. It's a bit beneath me.

Louise I'm sure you can lower yourself.

Sarah Right, I'll throw first. Come here. (*She moves to grab Louise*)

Louise Hang on. Use the crash mat.

Sarah I see you've learnt something, at least.

Louise pulls the mat c. *Sarah grabs Louise and throws her. Louise lands, gets up quickly and runs round to Sarah, ready to be thrown again*

Louise Again, throw me.

Sarah throws Louise again. Louise runs round as before

Come on, again ...

Sarah throws Louise five times, Louise getting quickly to her feet after each one and asking to be thrown again ... and again ... The final throw is more vigorous, though it is obvious that Sarah is becoming slightly tired

Sarah OK, fine, that's enough ...
Andy You're not even sweating, the pair of you.
Louise Right, my turn.
Sarah What?
Louise My turn to throw you.
Sarah I don't think so ...
Louise Come on.
Sarah No way.
Louise (*shouting*) Come on.
Sarah Don't shout at me.
Louise Andy?

Andy doesn't react. There is a moment's tension

  Stuart enters

Stuart What's all the shouting about?
Louise Nothing.
Stuart Bloody cold out there ...
Louise Yeh?

Stuart takes off his coat and shoes

Stuart Well they've done it — finally. Two months we've got ...
Andy It's gone through, has it?
Stuart Two months and we're out. I'm not one of your big boys, you see, not in the pockets of the bloody councillors. You know what I've heard today: Mathews, on the council, one of the big gobs — his sons train up at the sports centre, don't they, that's why he's not bothered about what's happening down here. It makes me bloody sick, it does. Anyway, let's have a good session — shake myself out of it.
Andy I'm out, Stuart — ankle's killing me.
Stuart That's useful — I was going to wipe the floor with you.
Sarah You probably would, the way he's going.
Stuart Well, Sarah, me and you. Sharpen you up.
Sarah No, I'm finished; me and Louise have had a big session, haven't we Louise?
Louise Yeh.
Stuart Oh, that's bloody great — I'll just go and fling myself at a bloody wall

in that case. I'll grab the rafters and go through some serious *Uchi* routine.
I could rip the bloody place to bits. It's got to me; I thought it hadn't, but
they've got to me. Sarah, you fancy your chances tonight?

Sarah Just going, Stu. Should've been here earlier.

Louise I'll stay, Stuart.

Stuart OK. Well, we'll have a light session. (*He shouts*) Bloody hell, I could
swing for that lot up at the council. You two might as well get off. Lounging
about like that in this weather, you'll end up in hospital.

Andy Yeh, right. Bloody freezing in here, Stu. No wonder they're trashing
it.

Stuart (*to Sarah*) When are you going for Black Belt?

Sarah When are the next gradings?

Stuart Two months. The nineteenth of November. You'll be my only entry.

Louise My birthday.

Stuart It'll be the last event that we hold here.

Andy Oh, it's not being held at Alderman Clough then?

Stuart The juniors are. I wouldn't go up there if they paid me. You're not
thinking of deserting me, are you?

Andy No. Not yet, anyway. (*He laughs*)

Sarah Right, I'll get my track suit. If you come up to our house, Andy, you
can get a shower ...

Stuart What's wrong with my showers?

Andy Bloody freezing.

Stuart You're getting soft, Brookesy.

Andy Many a true word ...

Sarah and Andy get their equipment together

Stuart Right, I'll just get warm. You OK?

Louise Yeh, fine.

Andy Right, Stu — see you when I see you.

Stuart Yeh.

Andy Tara, Louise, tara ...

Sarah Bye.

Sarah and Andy exit without ceremony

Stuart Don't forget Coventry.

Louise Why do you want her to fight for us?

Stuart I want one last champion from this club. You know what the clubs
are like: jealous. They didn't like it when we had Andy. If I get another
champion from here it'll get right up their nose.

Louise Whose nose?

Stuart Local clubs, Alderman's, Youth Centre, Scunthorpe — they don't
like it.

Louise Do you think I'll get my Brown Belt?

Stuart Should do, if you keep your head.

Louise Are Black Belt gradings any different, Stuart?

Stuart What happens at your Black Belt is: you fight three Brown Belts. If
you beat all three with *Ippon* you get a belt; if you beat two and one *Waazi*
you have to face a line-up. It's a tough job — if you don't. You have to wait
for the gradings to come around again. Why?

Louise Just asking.

Stuart Right. *Hajime.*

Louise *Hajime.*

They begin to grapple

She wouldn't train with me, said it was beneath her. Then she threw me on
the mat and refused to be thrown.

Stuart That's Sarah.

Louise Stand by, Stu. I'm going to launch you.

Stuart You just try.

Louise I will ...

Stuart I've got fifty pence says you won't — and you won't get Brown Belt.

Louise Fifty pence ... ?

Stuart Yeh.

Louise Big gambler.

Stuart It's all I've got.

Louise You're on.

Stuart And don't try *Tiaotoshi*, I've got that one.

Louise What about a foot sweep?

Stuart Never ...

Louise *Hari goshi*?

Stuart Not a chance ...

Louise What about this ... ?

Louise steps and turns and throws Stuart with a Tomenage, *he goes flying
over for* Ippon

Stuart (*prostrate*) Bloody hell ...

Louise *Tomenage.*

Stuart Where'd you get that from?

Louise I saw Karen Briggs do it.

Stuart Too right.

Louise I feel really comfortable with it ...

Stuart It's a winner. What about a pin afterwards?
Louise That's no problem.
Stuart You've really got into this, haven't you?
Louise Yeh.
Stuart Remember the first time?
Louise Don't remind me—I went home that night and started wrestling with my dad, he thought I'd gone light ...

There is a moment's silence. Stuart looks fed up

Are you all right, Stuart?
Stuart Yeh.
Louise Sure?
Stuart Fifteen years I've spent down here, fifteen years. Fifteen sodding years.
Louise Why are they closing it?
Stuart Well, it's not needed, is it — not with the new place. Everybody's going to go there, aren't they?
Louise Are you?
Stuart No chance. I'd rather die.
Louise They might ask you.
Stuart No, I'm not a favourite son; you see, I open my mouth.
Louise How do you mean?
Stuart Well, for a start: how long have you been coming here?
Louise About ten months.
Stuart Right: ten months and you're a Blue Belt.
Louise So ... ?
Stuart You've come through very quickly. You could be a Black Belt in, what, another four months — in some clubs you'd've still been doing break falls. I think you should dive in at the deep end. Some of the other lads don't like it that way, they think it's too dangerous. Especially for you lot.
Louise Women, you mean?
Stuart Ay. But I think, look, it's hard work, and the sooner you realize that the better. There's no short cuts — sooner or later you're going to have to hit the deck.
Louise Will it be in the Olympics?
Stuart Hope so, with the likes of Karen and Lorretta. They're bringing in that synchronized swimming. What next, darts?
Louise I'm not bad at darts, Stu. We could start a club.
Stuart Dunno.
Louise You could be my coach.
Stuart Do you reckon?
Louise Yeh, I'll buy some darts next week.

Stuart You're a right little nut case, aren't you?

Louise Me, yeh. I'm mentally unstable half the time. You know what I'm thinking about at the moment? I just fancy getting all dressed up and having a night down at *Peppermints*. Getting absolutely legless, picking some bloke up and sneaking him back home.

Stuart Sorry I can't oblige.

Louise I miss it.

Stuart I thought it bored you?

Louise I mean I can't believe it, I miss it.

Stuart Nobody's stopping you from doing what you want.

Louise Only me.

Stuart That's right.

Louise Maybe I'll treat myself then.

Stuart Good for the soul. My disco days are long past. You can tell me what it was like.

Louise (*changing tone*) Anyway. I'm bloody freezing, it's bitter in here.

Stuart Yeh. No heating. Sorry.

Louise That *Tomenage*, you didn't let me throw you, did you?

Stuart Did I buggery. You nearly broke my back. Oh yeh, here we are, by the way.

Stuart goes to his coat and produces a coin from the pocket. He flicks it to Louise

Louise What?

Stuart Fifty p.

Black-out

Music

SCENE 3

The Lights come up on the upper level; the music fades

Michele, wearing her evening disco gear, stands high above the dojo. *She almost looks like a prostitute, and might well be one. She is ebullient and full of energy and streetwise aggression. We should get a sense of the city, and urban violence*

Michele It's great out here, it is. It's what I fucking want. It's what I live for. The weekends: I can't wait till Friday night. All week cooped up, and then Fridays I'm free.

I love it. I love the danger of it. I love the sex of it. It's sexy, know what I mean, everybody's looking good. It's great.

You've got to live for now. You've gotta. No money in the bank and saving up for tomorra. Live for now, I mean there might not be a tomorra. It's now for me. Now, now, now.

I've got a shit-pit job, that's what I've got. I'm at somebody's beck and call all the time. I'm had, I am, all day at work, I'm had: "This burger's cold, this cup's stained, this table's filthy". They all have me. Have me running back and forward trying to please 'em.

But at night, oh yeh. Now that is different. I mean. I'm there.

I know what I've got; I like men to look, I can feel 'em looking, undressing me. I get all giggly and warm. I know they look, they're that chuffing thick. Just a tight pair of jeans or my pencil line skirt with black high heels — stupid twats going gaga ... I like a drink, a bottle of Pils; one or two and I'm teetering on the edge, in a bubble of my own — I feel like I'm sinking. I just go with it, falling ... I remember this teacher at school, stupid sod, all greased-back hair and bad breath; used to smell of cheap aftershave, so we bought him a bottle, he thought it was right nice — didn't know it was a joke. He was teaching Social and Moral Studies — what a joke, trying to teach me sex education: I've got a degree in it. He says, when young girls get pregnant it's because they fall under the feelings they have, they start to sink into their feelings. I thought what the hell is this stupid old sod on about, sinking — what's sinking got to do with gerring pregnant? But — when I've had a few bottles I'm sinking. I'm bloody well drowned ... I think when I'm with Steve, that's the best sort of sinking ...

I know — well — I know that people call me a bag an' that. They did at school, even the stupid teachers leered. I could see 'em out of the staffroom, leering: "Look at that, eh?" Sweaty jumpers and polyester trousers, that's teachers to me. So I'd flaunt it — lean over 'em, touch 'em. I've always been like that.

Staying in our house is like dying, like I'm in a chuffin' coffin and they're nailing me in. If I don't go out on the town, I'm dead. Hull's alive at weekend like nowhere I've been. *Hull Cheese, Bass House*, all the pubs are alive — *Shire Horse* ... It's brilliant, dangerous, funny: all the colours, and everybody in their shirt sleeves even when it's pissing it ... Hull at weekend, it's like Benidorm.

They're doing it: living. They're not boxed in, they're free, they feel great. I feel great — everybody feels chuffin' great ...

Loud disco music plays

Michele exits

Black-out

Scene 4

The dojo. *Later*

The Lights come up; the music fades

Louise and Stuart are finishing a groundwork session; both their bags are on stage with their tracksuits in them

Stuart is towelling down

Louise enters, looking rough and wiping her face with a damp cloth. We should notice she is now wearing a Brown Belt

Stuart (*looking at Louise*) Never again, eh? I say that every time I go out. Never again.
Louise My head's thumping.
Stuart Go home.
Louise I'll have to.
Stuart That'll teach you to drink.
Louise Sorry, Stu.
Stuart Was it a good night, after all that?
Louise What I can remember of it.
Stuart Bad, eh?
Louise I feel pathetic.
Stuart Did you "score" then?
Louise Don't.
Stuart So you didn't.
Louise I'm not saying.
Stuart So you did?
Louise (*a long remorseful sigh*) Oooohhh, Louise.
Stuart It's not that bad. Is it?
Louise It is.
Stuart Anybody I might know?

Louise I hope not. Oh God. What a bloody mess. (*She tries to shake off the dirt*) Ooohh. Awful. Sorry, Stu. I can't do any more tonight, my head's splitting.

Stuart I wanted to get off early anyway.

Louise Decorating, are you?

Stuart It's our Karen's birthday. Thirteen. She's having a big "do".

Louise Thirteen. Oh. That's when all the trouble starts.

Stuart Don't remind me.

Louise I was a bit of a late developer, I didn't start playing up until I was sixteen. And then suddenly I'd left school and I was supposed to be all grown up.

Stuart So last night was about making up for lost time, was it?

Louise I don't know what it was about really.

Stuart So I take it you're not stopping to do some weights?

Louise No.

Stuart Right. I've got to ferry all the kids home in my car.

Louise Yeh.

Stuart I'm like a bloody taxi service with our Karen.

Louise Responsibilities, eh? You know what the worse thing about last night was for me? I enjoyed it. I mean the parade, you know, the hunt. After that it's all the same, but the hunt's very exciting.

Stuart Yeh, well.

Louise Sorry.

Stuart Justifying it for yourself, aren't you?

Louise Maybe. This is the real me, Stu. Louise Underwood, sad case.

Stuart laughs. He understands, but can't help

During the following they put on track suits and prepare to leave. Silence

Stuart Well, we'll not have too many times down here now.

Louise No.

Stuart I'm keeping the mats — try and flog 'em.

Louise Do right.

Stuart I bloody am — and the weights.

Louise What about the crash mat?

Stuart Well I thought I'd keep that and one day build a raft and sail out of Hull. I'm not letting them sods have the benefit of 'em. We've worked hard for these mats, they're not having 'em. All the juniors have gone, you know ...

Louise Eh?

Stuart Nearly all my juniors have gone up there.

Louise Yeh?

Stuart Makes me want to spit.

Louise Not on your mats?

Stuart Yeh. No loyalty, that's the trouble with people today, no loyalty, you see. Part of the consumer world that is: they see money or sommat and they're off like rats up a drainpipe — whoooosh ...

Louise I've strayed.

Stuart You'll go up there, won't you — to Clough's — when we close?

Louise Dunno. I've been thinking about it.

Stuart You will.

Louise I'm thinking of throwing it in, especially how I feel.

Stuart You want to be ... my best little player throwing it in — that'll look great.

Louise What do you mean?

Stuart When we close you want to be going up to that Clough Sports Centre, fling 'em all over, and say things like: "Oh, yeh, you're not bad, but when I was training with Stuart Mason, that was sommat else", or "Yeh, Stuart Mason, best *Hari* I've ever seen. Oh, it was a great little club that Stuart ran". "Stuart? Taught me everything I know." That sort of thing. That's what I want you to do.

Louise You know what I've been thinking?

Stuart What?

Louise I'd like to have a shot at Black Belt.

Stuart I thought you were thinking of chucking it in?

Louise Yeh, but, you know? One final fling.

Stuart You're not ready.

Louise I think I am.

Stuart You're not.

Louise You've got to let me have a crack, Stu.

Stuart No.

Louise Yes.

Stuart You've come through too quickly. That standard, it's a bastard. Excuse my French.

Louise Look, you back me up — or there'll be no praise when I go up to Alderman Clough's.

Stuart You wouldn't stoop so low?

Louise Try me.

Stuart Do you think you can do it?

Louise I've got to go for it now.

Stuart I might have some bad news for you.

Louise What?

Stuart Goodwin's doing the same gradings. There'll probably only be a few there; all the others are grading up at Clough's.

Louise So what?

Stuart Are you still pissed? She's Dan standard.
Louise She can't make me feel any worse than I feel now, can she?
Stuart Listen, I'll support you — if you do one thing for me ...
Louise I'll try: what is it?
Stuart It's only a little thing.
Louise What is it?
Stuart No, I can't ask you.
Louise What is it?
Stuart If you enter the gradings ——
Louise Yeh.
Stuart Do me a favour.
Louise What?
Stuart Beat Sarah Goodwin — *for me...*

Music

Black-out

SCENE 5

The dojo

The Lights come up slowly; the music fades

The dojo *is at its most icy and depressed. A number of chairs or a bench are positioned by the side of the mat*

Andy and Sarah enter gingerly. Andy is wearing a sports blazer and looks every bit a champion. Sarah wears a track suit. They have never looked so fit

Sarah (*as she enters*) ... the point is she ran away. That's all I'm saying. Now maybe she would have run off and scarpered anyway, but she had been a regular attender and when something actually happened she got herself out of there. And that's what it's all about.

There is a silence. They both stand and look at the cold dojo

Andy It's still here then.
Sarah Not for much longer. He never did get that heating sorted.
Andy Too busy teaching self-defence.

Louise enters from the dressing room

There is a strong feeling of animosity in the air

Sarah You in the gradings?
Louise No, I'm here for a ballet lesson. (*She does a ballet movement*)
Sarah You'll wish you were.
Louise No, I am, honest. This is just a disguise.
Sarah Make the most of it; you'll not be smiling when I hammer you.
Andy Come on, you two ——
Louise Don't waste your breath.
Sarah I'll have you now.
Louise Grow up.
Andy Let's get changed.
Sarah Yes. There's a bad smell out here.
Louise (*shouting*) Yeh, it's my feet.

Andy and Sarah exit to the changing room

Louise gets on the floor and begins to do some leg-stretching exercises

Michele enters, looking very sheepish. She looks very rough, with no make-up. She carries a card and a bag with a large wrapped present inside it. She moves slowly to Louise

Michele Hey up ...

There is a silence

Louise D'you want?

Another silence

Michele Hey up ...
Louise I called. You're never in.
Michele Me mam said. At doctor's.
Louise You look ——
Michele Rough.
Louise Yeh.
Michele I'm up stick ...
Louise Chuffing hell ...
Michele Yeh ...
Louise Who?
Michele Dunno.

Louise gives a big sigh

I'm having it; my mam's gunna see to me.

Louise How are you?

Michele Oh, I'm well ... OK ...

Louise Do you want ... ?

Michele Yeh ... Keep me in ——

Louise Michele.

Michele What?

Louise (*meaning more than she can say*) Hey up ...

Michele Hey up ... Hey, here ... (*She gives the card to Louise*) Nearly forgot — Happy Birthday.

Louise Thanks a lot. (*She opens the card and reads it. There is a cartoon of judo players on the front of the card*) Nice verse.

Michele Gorrit for the picture.

Louise Good.

Michele Here, I've bought you this — didn't know what to get you ... (*She hands over the big parcel from her bag*)

Louise Oh Michele, you're daft.

Michele I know.

Louise What is it?

Michele Open it.

Louise opens the parcel, revealing a very very large judogi *top*

Louise It's brilliant.

Michele It wa' only size they had.

Louise Great.

Michele Put it on.

Louise puts it on. It is very big on her

Louise I'll wear it today. I've got my gradings. (*She swaps her old* judogi *for the new one*)

Michele I know. Saw Stuart thingy.

Louise Thanks a lot.

Michele Yeh.

Louise Thanks.

Michele (*taking the old top*) I'll keep this — might be a judo expert I'm having.

Stuart enters

Sarah and Andy come out of the dressing rooms and Sarah begins to warm up

Stuart (*seeing Louise in her new gear*) Bloody hell.
Louise My birthday present. Gunna see what it's like.

   Louise exits

Stuart (*to Michele*) You found her, did you?
Michele Yeh, thanks ...
Stuart (*to Andy*) Andy.
Andy Stuart.
Stuart All right?
Andy Not bad.
Stuart Good win in France.
Andy Cheers.
Stuart How's Sarah?
Andy Shit hot.
Stuart Looks good.
Andy I'm not exaggerating, Stuart — she'd beat me. How's your girl?
Stuart Louise.
Andy How is she?
Stuart She's OK.
Andy Well, all the best.
Stuart You've done it, Andy.
Andy Done what?
Stuart You've changed ...
Andy A change is as good as a rest, Stu, said that yourself ...

Sarah and Andy walk to the side of the mat

Sarah What did he say?
Andy Nothing.
Sarah What's she like?
Andy Fodder.
Sarah Good.
Andy Don't worry.
Sarah I feel a bit nervous.
Andy It's OK.
Sarah It's this place.
Andy You'll be fine.

   Louise enters

Stuart Get warm, you.
Michele It's bleeding freezing in here.

Louise and Sarah warm up, eyeing each other

Stuart takes the role of referee, standing C

The Lights fade, a spotlight picking out Stuart

Music

Stuart is full of tension: he must convey what has happened in the gradings before this final confrontation. He is full of anticipation

Stuart You fight for four minutes. Four minutes of total exhaustion, total dedication. Four minutes. The longest four minutes you'll ever live. A throw with force is *Ippon*, and victory. That's with impetus, on their back, smack. *Waza-ari* is almost *Ippon*, worth seven points, and *Yuko*, is almost *Waza-ari*, and then there's *Koka*. Bloody crazy, isn't it? It took me three years to work out the scoring. Now I don't even bother.

Sarah was on form. She came in and threw the big Scunthorpe girl for *Ippon*. Get down and out, hospital job. Louise twisted her hand against the girl from Driffield but Sarah ploughed over a girl from Leeds like she wasn't even there. Louise looked slow, sluggish; she really wasn't ready, I knew that, deep down I knew that. I let her go in and I knew she really wasn't ready. Then Goodwin came a cropper against the tall Driffield girl. So that was it. That was what I'd always feared. Louise would have to ace her. She was tired, she was weak, she was carrying a bad hand. She really didn't seriously stand a chance, and I knew that, deep in my heart: I knew she was going to get hurt.

The Lights return to their previous state

Andy Come on Sarah, straight in.
Michele Keep calm, Louise.
Andy Straight in.

The two girls stand

A good strong hold, she's easy.
Michele Remember, keep calm.
Andy Fodder, Sarah.
Michele Shurrup, you.
Sarah Going down, Underwood.
Louise No way.

Sarah Going down.
Louise Try me.
Stuart *Hajime!*

The girls grab each other, Sarah looking the stronger

Easy ...

Sarah grabs Louise's judogi and begins to pull very hard. Louise tries to grip on to Sarah

Easy ...

The girls turn three hundred and sixty degrees around the stage, fighting for grips. Sarah grips Louise powerfully

Louise Oh yeh ...
Sarah Look at this: no strength.
Andy Throw her.
Michele Smack her.

Sarah gets a good hold on Louise. She attempts a right handed Tiaotoshi, *which Louise steps out of. Sarah pushes Louise across the stage and catches her with* Ouchigari. *Louise falls to the floor. Sarah follows her to the floor and attempts to pin her with an approach from the* US *side — however Louise puts her head into Sarah's body and backs away. Sarah moves with her. Louise gets to her feet. This is a* matte *situation*

Michele Get up ...
Stuart *Matte!*

Both girls get up and stare at each other bitterly. During the following they redress their garments

Sarah I've got you.
Louise No way.
Andy *Hajime ...*

The girls begin to grapple once more C, *taking time to get a good grip. Louise foot-sweeps Sarah* DC *— unsuccessfully. Sarah pulls Louise* UC *and foot-sweeps her, catches her — and Louise bellies out on to the floor. Louise gets to her feet. They take up their positions*

Sarah You're going.

Louise Where?
Sarah Down.
Louise No chance, PC Plod ..

They grapple. Louise attempts Ippon Sieonage *and Sarah bellies out. They redress, then go for grips in a nice and slow grapple. Sarah tries* Harigoshi. *Louise blocks her. Sarah pulls on Louise's collar and Louise cart-wheels free. They go back to their starting positions for grips. Sarah crosses to Louise, throws her with* Osotogari, *and holds her in* Kesagetame. *Louise holds on to Sarah and they roll across the stage on to the red area*

Stuart Watch it, concentrate.
Andy Hold her.
Michele Shurrup, Brookes, or I'll smack you.
Andy ⎫ *(together) Matte*!
Stuart ⎭
Louise *(getting up from the floor)* You'll have to do better than that ...
Stuart Stop bloody talking and concentrate.
Louise I am.
Andy Stop messing about, Sarah: hit her, bang her over — she's nothing.
Michele Hey, I'll drop you in a minute.
Louise Sit down, Michele.
Stuart Hey you.

Sarah and Louise get ready to resume. Michele sits

Andy *Hajime ...*

The girls circle and grapple. Louise tries Ippon Sieonage *once more but it falls short and Sarah grabs her round the neck with her legs. Louise struggles to loosen the neck grip but Sarah rolls her over and begins to strangle her, trapping her face. Sarah, on her back, gets Louise on to her back*

Michele She's suffocating her ...
Stuart *Matte*!

Both girls stand. Louise rubs her face

Stuart Watch the face, Goodwin.

The girls face each other. They take holds on each other once more, circling, etc. Louise grabs Sarah hard and throws her for Tiaotoshi. *Sarah rolls out of the throw and on to her feet once more*

Once again they grapple for holds. Sarah takes hold of Louise's sleeve, then her collar and finally her neck. She takes hold of Louise's hair and, turning Louise DS away from Stuart, the referee, pulls on it

Louise Get off my hair!
Sarah (*quietly*) Shurrup.
Louise She's pulling my hair.

Sarah continues to pull Louise's hair; they move around the stage

Michele Get off her hair.
Louise Get off my hair.

Sarah lets go of Louise's hair and they face each other, Sarah R, Louise C

Sarah You're going this time, Underwood.
Louise Am I?

Louise attacks Sarah, grabs her and throws her over her head with Tomenage. Sarah lands on her back. It's agony. Suddenly the action goes into slow motion

Stuart Great bloody throw.

Music plays. Louise gets on to Sarah's back

Stuart On her — pull.
Michele Hold her ...

Louise gets Sarah into an arm lock and they roll upstage together

Stuart Pull.
Andy Hold it.
Stuart Pull.
Andy Hold on, wriggle.
Stuart Get her fingers.

Louise and Sarah roll back into position with Louise now firmly in the driving seat

Michele Pull her chuffin' arm off.

Louise pulls on Sarah's arm

Stuart Pull.
Michele Hold her ...

Sarah is strong and begins to pull back on the hold, gripping on to her own jacket. Louise attempts to loosen Sarah's grip (her intention being to force Sarah's arm out across Louise's body, thus breaking the arm and winning a submission)

Stuart Pull.
Andy Hold it.
Stuart Pull.
Andy Hold on ... wriggle about.
Stuart Get her fingers.
Michele Pull her chuffin' arm off.
Louise (*making a big attempt*) AAAAARRRRRRR ... !
Andy Hold, Sarah.
Stuart PULL!
Andy Hold it, she's fading, hold it.
Stuart Get her fingers, pull her fingers off.
Sarah You'll not do it ...
Louise No?
Sarah Never ...
Louise Arrrrrrr .... (*She pulls again*)
Sarah I'll never submit.
Louise Shut it.
Sarah Never.

Louise pulls Sarah's arm and gets her into the hold; she really puts the pressure on

Andy Sarah, submit.
Sarah No.
Andy She'll break your arm.
Sarah I'm not submitting ...
Louise Submit?
Sarah No.
Stuart Hang on to it, don't let go ...
Andy Submit.
Sarah No.
Louise Yes. (*She screams*) AAAAAARRRRRR!

Sarah screams. Louise puts the hold on harder

Sarah (*tapping submission*) I submit.

Louise still has the hold on

   My arm ...
Andy *Matte* ... MATTE ...

The action returns to normal speed and the music stops. Andy and Stuart move on to the mat. Louise is in tears

Michele Break her chuffin' arm off.
Andy Louise, she's tapped. She's submitted.
Stuart Louise ...

Louise releases Sarah, who lays still

Andy You've done it — let her go ...
Louise I'm knackered.
Stuart That was brill.
Louise Oh God, I feel sick.
Andy You all right, Sarah?
Louise I feel bloody ill ...
Michele Oh, it was great, Louise. God, aren't you hard?
Louise Oh God, I'm shagged.
Michele I am. Oh, listen to me.
Louise How's that for a favour, Stu?
Stuart Just right — just bloody right that.

There is a moment's silence. Andy gets Sarah to her feet

Louise You OK?
Sarah No.

Stuart produces a Black Belt

Stuart Here ...
Louise It's yours.
Stuart It's yours.
Louise Oh, God ...
Michele Put it on.
Louise (*putting on the Black Belt*) I'm crying ...
Michele Suits you.
Stuart It's great — looks good.

Louise Oh, thanks. I don't think I'll pack in, Stu ...
Stuart You stick at it.
Sarah Underwood ——
Louise What?
Sarah You're all right.
Louise Am I?

Michele produces Louise's snake belt

Michele Here, put this on and all ... (*She gives Louise the belt*)
Louise Oh — Snake Belt First Dan ...
Andy Well done.
Michele I'm right proud of you.
Stuart Me and all ...
Michele Louise?
Louise What?
Michele Hey up?
Louise Hey up ...

Michele and Louise laugh and hug each other; it's a touching moment

Music plays

The image freezes

CURTAIN

FURNITURE AND PROPERTY LIST

ACT I

On stage:　HIGHER LEVEL: PIPPINS
Tables
Chairs
Mop for **Louise**
Damp cloth for **Louise**

MAIN STAGE: DOJO
Large square of matting
Battered lockers
Splintered benches
Broken chairs
Large blue crash mat
Stuart's bag containing **Stuart**'s clothes, towel, balaclava

SCENE 1

Personal:　**Michele**: cigarettes and lighter
Louise: ring and necklace

SCENE 2

As before

SCENE 3

As before

SCENE 4

As before

SCENE 5

Off stage:　Towel (**Sarah**)
Stuart's bag containing **Stuart**'s clothes, etc.

SCENE 6

As before

SCENE 7

Set: MAIN STAGE
            Stuart's and Andy's sports bags containing track suits, running shoes,
                etc.

Off stage: Sports bag (**Louise**)

ACT II

Strike: Pippins set from higher level

Set: MAIN STAGE
            Dumb-bell

SCENE 1

Off stage: Large cassette player (**Louise**)

SCENE 2

As before

SCENE 3

Off stage: Sports bag (**Louise**)

SCENE 4

Set: Towel for **Stuart**
            Stuart's sports bag containing track suit
            Louise's sports bag containing track suit

Off stage: Damp cloth (**Louise**)

SCENE 5

Re-set: Chairs or bench at side of mat

Off stage: Card, bag containing wrapped judogi top (**Michele**)

Personal: **Stuart**: Black Belt
            Michele: Snake belt

LIGHTING PLOT

Practical fittings required: nil
A judo hall, *Pippins* hamburger restaurant, an empty space

ACT I, SCENE 1

To open: General interior lights on *Pippins*

Cue 1	Music	(Page 3)
	Black-out	

ACT I, SCENE 2

To open: General interior lights on judo hall

Cue 2	**Sarah**: "I fancy a drink ..."	(Page 17)
	Black-out	

ACT I, SCENE 3

To open: General interior lights on *Pippins*

Cue 3	**Michele** makes her way off	(Page 19)
	Black-out	

ACT I, SCENE 4

To open: General interior lights on judo hall

Cue 4	**Stuart** exits	(Page 21)
	Black-out	

ACT I, SCENE 5

To open: General interior lights on judo hall

Cue 5	**Stuart**: "I thought we were supposed to be training?"	(Page 29)
	Black-out	

ACT I, SCENE 6

To open: General interior lights on judo hall

Cue 6	**Michele** spits in **Louise**'s face	(Page 33)
	Black-out	

ACT I, Scene 7

To open: General interior lights on judo hall

Cue 7	**Louise** *mouths "Fucking hell!"*	(Page 39)
	Quick black-out	

ACT II, Scene 1

To open: General interior lights on judo hall

Cue 8	**Michele**: "Don't worry, I will do."	(Page 44)
	Black-out	

ACT II, Scene 2

To open: General interior lights on judo hall

Cue 9	**Stuart**: "Fifty p."	(Page 54)
	Black-out	

ACT II, Scene 3

To open: General exterior lighting on higher level

Cue 10	**Michele** exits	(Page 56)
	Black-out	

ACT II, Scene 4

To open: General interior lighting on judo hall

Cue 11	Music	(Page 59)
	Black-out	

ACT II, Scene 5

To open: Lights come up slowly to general interior lighting on judo hall

Cue 12	**Stuart** stands c	(Page 63)
	Fade lights except spot on **Stuart**	
Cue 13	**Stuart**: "I knew she was going to get hurt."	(Page 63)
	Return lights to their previous state	

EFFECTS PLOT

ACT I

Cue 1   **Michele** exits   (Page 3)
Music

Cue 2   The lights come up   (Page 4)
Fade music

Cue 3   Black-out   (Page 19)
Music

Cue 4   The lights come up   (Page 20)
Music

Cue 5   **Stuart**: "I just want to stay here."   (Page 21)
Music

Cue 6   The lights come up   (Page 21)
Fade music

Cue 7   Black-out   (Page 29)
Music

Cue 8   The lights come up   (Page 29)
Fade music

Cue 9   Black-out   (Page 32)
Music

Cue 10   The lights come up   (Page 33)
Fade music

Cue 11   Quick black-out   (Page 39)
Music

ACT II

Continue interval music under beginning of scene; fade music on house speakers and play through Louise's cassette player when ready

Cue 12	Black-out *Music*	(Page 44)
Cue 13	The lights come up *Fade music*	(Page 44)
Cue 14	Black-out *Music*	(Page 54)
Cue 15	**Michele**: "— everybody feels chuffin' great ... " *Loud disco music*	(Page 56)
Cue 16	The lights come up *Fade music*	(Page 56)
Cue 17	**Stuart**: "Beat Sarah Goodwin — *for me* ... " *Music*	(Page 59)
Cue 18	The lights come up *Fade music*	(Page 59)
Cue 19	**Stuart**: "Great bloody throw." *Music*	(Page 66)
Cue 20	**Andy**: "*Matte* ... MATTE ... " *Fade music*	(Page 68)
Cue 21	**Michele** and **Louise** hug each other *Music*	(Page 69)

PRINTED IN GREAT BRITAIN BY
THE LONGDUNN PRESS LTD., BRISTOL.

Lightning Source UK Ltd.
Milton Keynes UK
UKHW02f1423131018
330487UK00005B/144/P